COVER CREDIT: For details of
our cover picture supplied by
John Hannavy, turn to page 6

This quarterly *Country Origins* is part of the service provided by The Countrylover's Club of Great Britain & Ireland, PO Box 4, Nairn IV12 4HU. Tel: 01667 454441. Fax: 01667 454401. *Country Origins* is sent automatically to Club members but you may subscribe to it (or give gift subscriptions) individually. Editorial contributions are welcome, but please study the magazine carefully or send a sae for Notes to Contributors. Contributions will not be acknowledged unless a stamped postcard is provided, and should be accompanied by a sae for their return if desired. Please write and do not telephone on editorial matters. Note that the best articles are generally those with real information (and actual fact), and that suitable photographs (black and white or colour) greatly enhance the chances of publication. Neither

the editor, Hilary Gray, nor the publishers can accept responsibility for material submitted. Unless you state otherwise the Club reserves the right to publish material submitted in any of its titles.

*Country Origins* is published on the second Thursday of March (spring), June (summer), September (autumn) and November (winter). It is distributed to the news trade by Diamond. Typesetting is by Posthouse Printing & Publishing, The Park, Findhorn, Forres, Moray IV36 0TZ. The printer is Cradley Print Ltd, Chester Road, Cradley Heath, Warley, West Midlands B64 6AB.

The advertising manager is Wendy Goodman, 3 Marlborough Drive, Ringswell Park, Middlemoor, Exeter EX2 5QE. Tel: 01392 213894. Fax: 01392 493228.

# Collecting the Countryside

*John Hannavy*

*I COULD not resist sending this to you for your album. Is it worthy of a place? He's got such a Kent-like face, hasn't he? JM*

So went the message on a postcard sent to a Mr J. McWillie of Rock Ferry on 21 March, 1907. The postcard, printed from a carefully tinted black and white photograph, showed a farm-hand standing beside his sturdy and majestic cart horse – although it has to be said the horse seems to

5987          *Welsh Fisherwomen*

**Our cover picture of Welsh fishwives on the rocks with their shrimp baskets was published in this form about 1906 hand-tinted and reproduced using lithography – but the women shown in the picture may well have all been long dead by the time the card appeared. They had, in fact, posed for the picture some thirty years earlier. The original image had been taken by a photographer working for Francis Frith of Reigate in the 1870s, and published as one of Frith's many thousands of British views designed to be pasted into the Victorian photo album. It is an interesting commentary on the unchanging nature of country life in late Victorian Britain, that the scene had not become outdated in all that time. The location is believed to be Tenby.**

The Ploughman.

*Overleaf*: **Postcard from 1907, one of a huge number of farming views published as postcards between 1905 and the outbreak of the First World War. The sender described the ploughman as having a 'Kent-like face'.**

have been a lot more interested in the camera than the farmer was!

The message often took second place to the image – the usual reason for sending the card being the gift of the picture itself. And yet, the sender invariably felt obliged to add some message to personalise the whole procedure – with words often chosen with less than careful thought! One postcard of a group of piglets with their noses in the trough, sent to an address in Leeds in 1906, bore the message 'Hope you are as busy as these are, Davy'.

Postcards, as we know them today, are a product of the years around the turn of the century. Before that time, only the address was permitted on the reverse of the card. A message, if one was added, was written over the picture, or on a small section of the illustrated side left blank for that purpose. It was only in 1901 that the British Post Office permitted a message on the same side as the address – although in terms of etiquette, sending messages of any sort by postcard was still considered a rather inappropriate activity for the upper classes.

Collecting postcards was a turn-of-the-century craze, enjoyed by many thousands, and fuelled by several times that number of different cards. Promoted with the help of the recently introduced halfpenny post, there was hardly a middle class household in the country without a postcard album.

Collecting postcards, however,

*Left*: **Hand-tinted carte de visite photograph from the 1870s, photographer unknown. The tradition of collecting carte de visite photographs began in the late 1850s when the Parisian photographer Disderi was permitted by Napoleon III to market his carte de visite portrait commercially.**

*Opposite*: **Studio portrait, photographer unknown. Pit Brow lasses worked the coal screens in Lancashire mines and Welsh mines. They sorted the coal from the stone, picking lumps of stone off conveyor belts at the pit head all day long. The girls preferred this to working in the damp warmth of the cotton mills – believing that, despite the coal dust, working out of doors in all weathers was much more healthy. This card dates from 1904 or 1905, and the girls worked at Pemberton Colliery, Wigan. Pages 10 and 11: Pit brow Girls at Junction Colliery, Wigan, 1904.**

PIT BROW GIRLS 1.

predates by many years the introduction of the photographic postcard as we know it. Beautiful hand engraved and printed cards were available in the 1860s so, by the advent of the photographic card, collecting was a well established hobby.

Postcards were produced as a celebration of British landscape and architecture – as today – but those represented the tip of the iceberg in terms of numbers. In the days before illustrated newspapers and magazines, the days before film and television held sway, and in an age when a journey to the next town or city might still have been considered something of an expedition, the postcard was one of the keys which revealed the mysteries of unseen places, unknown cultures, and everyday occupations. Postcards fulfilled an important role in broadening understanding of the lives people lived in other parts of the country.

Nothing was considered too specialist or too trivial as a subject for a postcard. The crafts and occupations of people throughout Britain were celebrated on a scale which the previous collecting craze – the *carte de visite* photograph – had never attained.

But it was the lowly carte de visite – that small print the size of the Victorian visiting card – which had established the collecting habit in the 1860s and 1870s, and which, to a considerable extent, had established the idea of using the collected image as a means of quietly educating the collectors!

As early as the 1860s, British working people – the village blacksmith, the farmer, and the fisherman were as familiar as subjects for photography as the Queen and her Prime Minister.

The ideas for the pictures did not always come from the photographers, however. The eccentric Arthur Munby, obsessed by Victorian working women in the 1850s and 1860s, actually commissioned local photographers to produce studies of working women – from the pit brow lasses of Wigan to the fisher girls of the Yorkshire Coast, and from the serving girls of the great stately homes throughout the country, to music hall and circus performers wherever he found them. His fascination – coming from a background where women were considered largely decorative – was with the contrasts between these women at work, and the very different and conventionally feminine image they portrayed at home.

Many other photographers saw a market in images of local customs, traditions and costumes. Their pictures, shot speculatively, were sold wholesale to photographers and print sellers nationwide, who in turn sold them on to their local customers.

For some, the format was the carte de visite, while for others it was the 3-D photograph, designed to be viewed in the drawing room stereoscope.

To meet the growing demand for such images, many of the leading photographers of the day took photographs of local crafts, local traditions, and local employment. Their images were often sold as stereoscopic cards, as cartes de visite, or as larger views to be pasted into the Victorian scrapbook.

In all probability, every area had

Farm Life - Carrying...

postcards based on local crafts, customs and occupations. Seeing them side by side offers interesting comparisons of dress and equipment. In mining photographs, the greatest distinction between one area and another was dress – in Wigan the pit brow lasses wore breeches, while in nearby Haydock, the wearing of trousers was considered likely to inflame their male workmates, and the wearing of 'kirtles' – long skirts – was therefore required.

Each colliery had its own 'uniform' for the girls who worked on the coal screens so there might have been as many postcards as there were collieries.

The postcard of Newhaven fishwives (page 14) dates from about the same time as the publication of the Welsh example – about 1907 – and the differences in dress, the shape of creels and so on, are what made each area of mainland Britain distinctive.

**From about 1910, this lightly coloured card follows an already well established tradition of rural subject matter**

Interestingly, while the Newhaven women were photographed in the studio, in the older Welsh picture – in the 1870s, the sensitivity of photographic plates was much lower – the use of a natural outdoor location was preferred by Frith's cameraman.

Today with postcards carefully taken to exclude anything which might date them – cars, people, fashions – the real character of the British landscape, both urban and rural, is distorted beyond recognition. The Edwardians knew that it was people, and their pride in their work, which gave life to the picture postcard, and made it worth collecting.

*Overleaf*: **This studio portrait of a group of Lothian fisherwomen with their creels and their produce dates from about 1906.**

# Driven Crazy!

## *David Watkins* has some examples of the humorous side of the postcard industry...

IT is exactly a hundred years ago since the motor car made its first appearance in this country.

Indeed, it was J.E. Knight of Franham who produced the very first British-built motor car propelled by internal combustion and exhibited it at the Crystal Palace Show in 1896.

Early motor cars of the time were to be treated as subjects of humour, but soon people of the countryside in particular had to adapt themselves to a new manifestation of speed as motorists raced along country roads at speeds which often exceeded 20 mph.

These primitive cars with their gas headlamps and solid tyres were derisively termed 'horseless carriages', but very soon the public was to become accustomed to all kinds of distressing car accidents – throughout the countryside in particular.

Cars were often found upside down in ditches and wrapped around tree trunks. Country dwellers were knocked down, run over and were vociferously threatened by angry drivers, whilst horses and farm animals were easily frightened by the sudden appearance of cars and fled in panic.

Hullo ! Had an Accident ?
No, you Fool, I'm Picking Blackberries

You can come out now,
it's geen o'er raining!

FROM "PUNCH." "WHERE IGNORANCE IS BLISS," &c.

He (alarmed by the erratic steering): "Er – and have you driven much?"
She (quite pleased with herself): "Oh, no – this is only my second
attempt. But then, you see, I have been used to a bicycle for years!"

One of the artists of the time who recorded such incidents in a humorous way was Lance Thackeray, who was employed by Messrs Raphael Tuck & Sons, later to become the largest producers of postcards in Britain.

Thackeray tirelessly pedalled off into the countryside on a bicycle which had been adapted to carry his easel, paints and other paraphernalia.

Another prominent artist of the time who featured car humour in his postcard illustrations was John Hassell. He was for some time an employee of *Punch* magazine, and the most famous car postcard that he ever produced is that of a motorist proceeding in the countryside with a rod attached to the steering wheel with a bunch of carrots at its end. The postcard reproduced in many books, is aptly entitled 'Persuasion is better than force'.

Women drivers did not escape unscathed. The spirit of the time is evident in a 'Where Ignorance is Bliss' postcard showing a motor car driven by a woman, narrowly avoiding collision with a horse-drawn carriage in a country lane:

He (alarmed by the erratic steering): 'Er – and have you driven much?'

She (quite pleased with herself): 'Oh, no – this is only my second attempt. But then, you see, I have been used to a bicycle for years!'

Special motoring clothes were absolutely essential since the driver and passenger were exposed to the mud, dust and stone chippings from untarred roads in the countryside.

Goggles were worn by all since the eyes had to be protected from flying stones and horse-shoe nails, and in the summer from clouds of dust.

Women would also wear a face-mask lined with soft leather since they feared that the complexion would be ruined by the harsh countryside winds. Alternatively, women could wear a veil, and often this apparel was considered more feminine since few were ready to disfigure themselves so hideously in public by wearing goggles over the eyes.

The veil, which might be made of crêpe de chine, was at least two yards long, passing over the hat and tying in a becoming bow under the chin. When the dust became unsufferable, it was pulled over the face.

Cold was a real problem for early motorists. Bearskins were worn by the more fashionable drivers, but such coats had their problems since they held dust easily and became muddy indeed as cars bumped their way along dusty country lanes or through puddles.

The motorist's strange clothing was often a subject for mockery, as illustrated in one instance where two very inquisitive country lads peer under the bearskin coat of a proud motorist standing beside his car. They innocently remark:

'It must be somewheres'
'Wot must?'
'Wy its tail'

In another:

'You can come out now, it's geen o'er raining!' says a rustic to a driver in peaked cap and goggles, as he

"It must be somewheres"
"Wot must?"
"Wy its tail."

"POOR FELLOW, HERE'S A PENNY FOR YOU-NOW PLAY 'HOME SWEET HOME!'"

Persuasion is better than force.

COPYRIGHT ENT'D AT STAT. HALL.

MOTOR STATISTICS.

Joan: "What be the meanin' o' that number 'anging up in front ?"
Darby: "Why, that be the number o' people they've killed."

emerges oil-spattered from 'underneath'.

In a scene where an antiquated couple gaze in amazement at an early car in their village the dialogue goes:

Joan: 'What be the meanin' o' that number 'anging up in front?'
    Darby: 'Why, that be the number o' people they've killed.'

*Joanna Toye, author of our article on the facing page, was until last year Senior Producer of* **The Archers.** *Her novel,* **Shula's Story***, containing new material, is now available in paperback, published by Penguin Books, price £5.99.*

# Behind the Scenes

## The second part of our *Archers* series by Joanna Toye

WHEN Norman Painting was offered the part of Phil Archer, he was a busy freelance writer, actor and producer, working for the BBC Midland Region. 'It seemed new and interesting,' he wrote in his 1984 autobiography *Reluctant Archer*, 'and it would only take two and a half days a week.' What Norman did not know then, and nor did anybody, was that it would take up 45 years of his life!

These days, the cast record for six days a month in Studio Three at the Pebble Mill Studios in Birmingham. The studio is divided into three. There is a carpeted area which serves for interiors – the cosiness, of Glebe Cottage or the grandeur of Grey

**The programme's first Editor, Godfrey Baseley, was a stickler for authenticity. Here the BBC's 'mobile recording vehicle' is pictured at Maxstoke, near Coventry, getting the lowdown on hurdle-making.**

*Opposite above:* **When** *The Archers* **began Tony Shryane was given the combined job of sound engineer and junior producer.** He trawled the countryside for appropriate sound effects, never afraid to boldly go where no microphone had been before!

*Opposite below:* **As sound engineer and producer Tony Shryane himself controlled the sound quality of the early episodes. Though the mixing desk looks as if it belongs in the Science Museum, 'The Archers' swiftly became so popular that is displaced 'Dick Barton', the popular detective series on which it had been modelled.**

Gables can be created by moving screens to give a bigger or smaller acoustic. Part of the carpeted area, the so-called 'sink', since it has a working sink in it, is used for kitchen scenes and also for the bar of The Bull. Then there's an area with a hard floor, which can be Pat's dairy or the village hall or, with the addition of some straw on the floor (actually scrap recording tape), becomes the cowshed or the lambing shed. Then there's the 'dead' area, a cubby-hole of dead acoustic into which any sound effect can be played to create an exterior – Lakey Hill, the village green or the road where Mark Hebden had his fatal car crash.

Each fifteen-minute episode takes two and a quarter hours to record with the latest digital technology – which is twice the pace of other radio dramas. New actors joining the cast have a steep learning curve, but it can't be as terrifying as the studio 45 years ago when episodes of *The Archers* were transmitted live! An actor who was late for the studio could throw the whole recording into

---

### Alec Phillips of Ayrshire writes:

NOT just decades ago... but now more than a century. How I wish I had taken more heed of the things my father told us children about his country life.

Born in 1872, he went to farm work in Manuden in Essex as half-timer at the age of eight. Scaring birds was part of his work, a lonely job for such a young child. In later years he did all manner of farm work – ploughing, sowing by hand, threshing corn with a 'stick-and-a-half' and so on.

My own recollections include how we as children would go gleaning for corn to feed the family chickens.

One method of threshing was to put the ears of corn in an old sock which was laid on the ground and beaten with sticks. The corn was winnowed by the age-old method of throwing the beaten product into the air in a light breeze so that the grains of corn fell straight down and the husks blew away. Gleaning wheat was fine – we pulled off the straw and put the heads into our lap bags. But barley was not so good because the awls were so unpleasant. However, we certainly enjoyed the eggs our parents got from the chickens. There were happy carefree days for us children but very hard for our parents and their fellow farm workers.

Tony Shryane talks through the script with an expectant (and somewhat mischievous-looking) cast. Front row (left to right) Joy Davies (Mrs Fairbrother), Anne Cullen (Carol Grey), Lesley Saweard (Christine Archer), Gwen Berryman (Doris Archer), Leslie Dunn (Paul Johnson). Back row: Leslie Bowmar (Mr Fairbrother), Norman Painting (Phil Archer), Harry Oakes (Dan Archer) and Denis Folwell (Jack Archer).

disarray, and Patricia Greene, who plays Jill, tells the story of one fellow actor who got on the wrong train in London. It was a through train which didn't stop at Birmingham. As it sped on through Wolverhampton and the Black Country, he resorted to wrapping notes around anything that came to hand and flinging them on to the track, hoping they would be picked up. The notes read: 'Am on non-stop train to North West and can't make it

1964 and there's a new face among the cast: Monte Crick (back, left) took over from Harry Oakes as Dan. Also shown, left to right: Gwen Berryman (Doris Archer), Anne Cullen (Carol Grenville), Norman Painting (Phil Archer) and the tireless Tony Shryane. Norman is leaning against the 'spot door' which can be wheeled to various parts of the studio to help to create entrances and exits, the rattle of bolt and chain and of keys in the lock.

to 'Archers' studio. Tell Godfrey Baseley!' Luckily, someone did.

Live recordings were nothing new to Norman Painting, who had begun broadcasting professionally in his last year at University when producers were not averse to making cuts in the script when the programme was actually on the air, by the simple method of walking into the studio, leaning over an actor's shoulder and crossing out the lines which were to be removed from further down the page! Luckily he was among fellow professionals – and friends, like Bob Arnold (Tom Forrest), whose radio career began when, billed as 'Bob Arnold, The Farmer's Boy' he sang the folk songs for which he had acquired a reputation in the pubs around his home town of Burford.

In the early days, many of the cast were not professional actors at all, but real country folk. George Hart, who played Jethro Larkin, was from a famous family of Chipping Camden silversmiths. And of course there was the late Mollie Harris, well known for her country reminiscences (and among the cast and production team for her generous supplies of her home-made wine!) whose Martha Woodford was a country character through and through.

One of the most exciting early broadcasts was one in which even the cast didn't know the content of the scripts until the very last minute. Under the pretence of 'topicality', scripts for the evening episode on 22nd September 1955 were not distributed and it was only when the cast arrived at the studio that they learnt that a character was to be killed off that night. The victim was Grace Archer (Ysanne Churchman) and the date of her death was no coincidence – it was the night that ITV was to start transmission. Who says the ratings wars are anything new?

Grace's tragic death (to really turn the screw, she died trying to save Christine's horse, Midnight, from a stables fire) wiped all mention of ITV from the front pages of the next day's newspapers and the BBC's switchboard was jammed with callers who were alternately irate and distressed. But the story had a happy ending. Two years later, Phil married Jill, and had four children. Later still, Ysanne Churchman returned to the programme to play gravel-voiced Mary Pound – something which could never happen on television!

---

### Caught Out

IN the 30s, the men never did household shopping, only buying items for the farm or the animals. One day, Jack Oliver, a shepherd from Fleehope, went into Wooler. In the market place was Miss McEwen's hardware shop. It was a good little shop but Miss McEwen was very slow and could never find anything. Jack Oliver's patience wore thin. 'Hurry up, Miss McEwen, I need a mousetrap, I have to catch a bus!' 'Ay Mr Oliver,' she said in all seriousness, 'I don't sell mousetraps to catch buses.' – *Bunty Cowe*

# Summer Saturdays in the West

### David St John Thomas

REMEMBER the days when the train journey was the best part of the holiday? Mum might have worried about getting all the luggage on board, dad about getting his corner seat and also a place in the restaurant car. But for the young, making a foray further from home than ever before, it was usually sheer magic.

It did, however, rather depend on which day you travelled. Always known as the holiday line, the Great Western (and its successor the Western Region) almost always had the perfect ambience, apart from overcrowded summer Saturdays. On

those days, huge crowds descended on the South West at the same time – especially the peak fortnight straddling the old Bank Holiday weekend at the beginning of August (discussed in the last Country Reporter).

Summer Saturdays in the West are words that still evoke nostalgia for railway enthusiasts. This reporter indeed even wrote a book by that very title, and it surprised everyone by racing through successive editions. Especially on 'the' day, going down the first Saturday of the peak fortnight and returning two weeks later, the operation was conducted in pure military style. Analysing the performance made wonderful copy for the regional Sunday and the next day's *Western Morning News*. Nearly always it was the front-page lead, combining that magic ingredient every editor seeks: involvement of a large proportion of their readership (since one way or another most people were linked to tourism, and in most families someone's working hours were linked to railway timetables. The subject combined railways, the local economy and even social behaviour.

For the reporter, getting a picture of what was happening usually meant sticking by a phone rather than seeing the action in person. Key railwaymen from around the system could be phoned, or would phone in their own reports. Stationmasters at the resorts were anxious for their performance to be shown up in a good light, and even an occasional engine driver would call with his own version. And on Sunday morning the stationmasters of key stations were instructed to report how many long-distance passengers had been received by the respective routes. In those days the Western routes included Paddington, intermediate stations to Bristol and also South Wales, Birmingham London Midland, the Western's own North Warwick line to the Midlands, and the North via Severn Tunnel and Shrewsbury.

Many trains ran in several portions, sometimes five, though there was only track allocation for one or two. Many Midlands and Northern industrial towns and even suburbs were starting points for trains to Torbay or Cornwall. The procession began in the early hours of Saturday morning, most trains returning visitors home at the end of their holiday having travelled down overnight. If they arrived late – and frequently the average delay was 120 minutes – the returning services also started late. Stations like Paignton and Torquay might then be besieged by thousands of waiting passengers, kept outside in the rain on wet summer Saturdays which seemed pretty common.

Every available locomotive, goods and passenger, was pressed into service, delaying the average speed. Many trains were allowed an hour or more above their mid-week timings. Rolling stock included many ancient vehicles, even four-wheeled carriages (without bogies) being common immediately after the war.

These were the days when you had either a full restaurant car meal or no refreshments at all. A whole train-full

**A typical 1957 summer Saturday's train (the locomotive displaying a three figure identification code for the benefit of signalmen in pre-computer days; this is a Plymouth-Liverpool express) nearing Dawlish. Seldom were coaches of the same style, or even livery, in uniform sets.**

of restaurant cars was worked down from Paddington on Saturday night, their crews dossing down in the offices over the booking hall (later taken over by David & Charles at Newton Abbot railway station) before working back on separate trains next day. More restaurant cars passed through Newton Abbot on summer Saturdays than ran in the whole of Italy. So that up to five sittings could be crowded in, the summer Saturday fare was cold meat and salad (laid out on the table before passengers came in) and ice cream and fruit, coffee extra.

Over 30,000 passengers from at least as far away as Bristol arrived at Torquay and Paignton, and over 6,000 were taken up the winding, hilly Newquay branch. Exeter St David's sometimes had over 10,000 passengers on it or within waiting trains. You had to queue before getting anywhere near the ticket barriers.

The story was always the same. Passengers from Paddington (remodelled in the 1930s especially for summer Saturday traffic) had a fine journey until they approached Taunton, as did most from the Midlands north and south via Bristol. At Taunton the two routes merged, only one pair of rails rising over the summit at Whiteball Tunnel on the Somerset/Devon border. Often trains then stopped at every signal to Exeter and Newton Abbot, where the Torbay line sometimes stretched back to Dawlish, and delayed trains for Plymouth and Cornwall. Local passengers had a raw deal, their trains occupying valuable track space often

running hours late; eventually many local services were replaced by buses on the busiest days.

In these pre-computer times, the pressure of telephone and paperwork in the control offices was intense. Signalmen frequently lacked time to eat. Every locomotive displayed its special three-number code to help identification, but mistakes were frequent. One engine driver stopped his train on the through (platformless) track at Exeter St David's opposite this reporter holding his copy of the day's working arrangements to ask: 'Shouldn't I be stopping here; what shall I do?' A hasty dash to the control office resulted in the train pulling forward and being backed (all fifteen carriages) into the down platform.

The Southern was just as busy, its platforms at Exeter St David's never empty for more than a couple of minutes as each of the North Devon and North Cornwall termini sported their own full-length independent trains, often again with restaurant cars. Newcomers such as the Surbiton-Okehampton car-carrying train also had to be accommodated. Not a goods truck moved on a peak summer Saturday.

Each year the railways carried greater crowds, but sadly the heroic efforts were not just in vain, they actually delayed progress. As long as people could travel on the peak days, they would. Only when many switched to driving, and found themselves in endless queues, did the thought of staggering holidays really take root.

The story of the great traffic jams might be for a later *Country Origins*.

Once it took six hours to drive from Brixham to Honiton. With screaming children and overheating engines, that was not endurable. Steadily people extended their travel periods, both within the week and over the season as a whole. The traffic jams made more difference than any government legislation or preaching, and in hindsight it is sad that all that super effort made by the railwaymen of the 1950s actually delayed the trend to a longer holiday season, which in turn paved the way for higher standards. For as long as up to a third of the total season's visitors arrived on a single day, and much accommodation was only occupied for four or five weeks in total, there was absolutely no inducement to invest in things like en-suite bathrooms.

**Footnote.** Not only did the railways bring in the majority of the ever-increasing holiday crowds, the peak of Saturday business not being reached until 1958, but the car-less visitors mainly travelled around their chosen area by train. Many used Runabout tickets, allowing unlimited journeys within a prescribed area. Local traffic was often extremely heavy, some local trains in the South Devon area having a dozen or more carriages, and even then occasionally passengers had to be left behind.

During the peak fortnight, many local people also travelled with Runabout Tickets or took half-day excursions. For example, on Sundays over 6,000 passengers sometimes travelled from Exeter St Thomas (not the city's main station) solely to Dawlish Warren.

There were also the days of the City of... trains. For an inclusive fee, and given the same reserved seat, passengers went to ten different destinations during the fortnight.

---

### The Train Now Standing...

IN their last days, many branch-line trains carried more railway enthusiasts than ordinary passengers. Guards were usually cooperative, maybe asking if a young traveller would prefer to switch to first class or ride on the engine, and often agreeing to delay the return departure by a few minutes to allow longer to look round the village or market town at the terminus.

On an otherwise empty train in Mid-Wales, one enthusiast said he had run out of film. The guard held the train at a platform at the head of the village street, half way down which was a chemist. Rushing into the shop, out of breath, the traveller was abruptly told to wait his turn. With the chemist engaged in social chit chat, eventually he exploded: 'My train is waiting for me!'

The chemist and the other customers took some convincing and the lad was only served after they had all trotted out on to the pavement and seen the train halted on the bridge at the street's head.

## REFLECTIONS

# Life on the Farm

**Corn harvesting in West Wales**

HOW many farmers nowadays would know the rules for harvesting in sheaves, should the necessity arise? Could they walk through a crop and judge by the colour of the straw and

**The early Fordson Major, the Galloping Major, pulling a corn binder. A single tow bar replaced shafts on what was a horse-drawn machine. The back rider adjusted height of sails and cutting-bed, and reported sail or twine breakages. Several lengths might be driven before shouts penetrated machine noise to remedy this.**

grain, and the feel of the grain, whether or not it was ready to cut?

Very little skill or knowledge is required to judge when corn and weather are right for combining. Grain must be ripe and dry, then a whole year's crop can be cut, threshed and in store within the day.

Combines can save grain that is so ripe it sheds at a touch, but corn to be gathered in by the flailing sails of a binder, thrown on to the conveyer sheet, sorted and packed into sheaves which are then thrown back on the field, must have sturdy, flexible straw and secure heads of grain.

Barley ripens first. Stalks crack and the heads of long-whiskered seeds nick over. Oats are next, the husks beginning to gape as the grains ripen. Both crops must be fully grown but still slightly green. It was the custom in West Wales to grow barley and oats together so that the longer-stalked oats could support the much shorter barley when the weather was battering it into the ground. A

**Oats and barley being stocked**

compromise had to be made over cutting to allow for the difference in ripening times.

Wheat was cut last, not ripening until late August. One of the signs to look for was colouring in the straw: green at the bottom, shading into red, then gold at the top. Grains from the three crops were tested for plumpness and they also had to contain a milky fluid. This fluid hardens into flour when the grain is fully ripe.

Wheat was grown here only to government order. It did not produce a quality grain, soil and climate being too poor, but the War-Ag never managed to deduce from this that it was pointless to insist on the regulation two acres or so intended for national consumption.

All crops were cut two or three weeks earlier than combining is done.

The binder is a very clever machine. It makes sheaves with a sloping foot so that two will lean inwards together on a firm base. If the first two sheaves would not stand firm together without further support, then the whole stock would be weak. Four sheaves placed pyramid fashion was customary in this area for a stook, or sometimes six pairs in a line.

Each sheaf was tied with the knot on the long side. This was of great significance. It gave quick guidance on how to pick up and place sheaves in the stook and did the same for building the load on a cart and making a stack. The slope of the foot made the sheaves stack together well and also formed a slope to encourage rain to run off. The knot was also helpful at threshing time when cutting and feeding sheaves into the drum. The strings were kept and used to tie sacks of grain, and other useful things.

Sheaves needed to stand and ripen for two to three weeks before being carted and stacked to await threshing. That was in ideal conditions – but these almost never existed, of course. To have three weeks without rain at any time of year was quite remarkable; to have it at harvest time would be miraculous. The tightly bound centre was the last to dry and if this was wet the stack would heat and the grain would rot. Clean straw would have dried more quickly but weeds were abundant and these were green and juicy. Many of them were also prickly. Testing involved thrusting the hand into a representative number of sheaves and hands and fingernails became tender with thistle thorns.

Stooking had to be redone many times, but it was not only after strong winds that this was necessary. There were few things in a cow's life so enjoyable as getting into a field of stooked corn – and there were few things in a farmer's life so infuriating, frustrating and exhausting as trying to get them out.

Up and down the rows, heads and udders swinging, they chewed, tossed and kicked. The game was to demolish as many stooks as possible, and it was hilarious. Even the humans had to laugh at least once through their fury and breathlessness to see these normally stately, rather cumbersome animals kicking their heavy hindquarters in the air or standing like cartoon duchesses with a floppy straw hat drooping from a horn and another straw, like a fag, from the mouth.

To protect the vulnerable seedheads from the weather, field-mows were built, small stacks of fifty to sixty sheaves each. These kept grain dry in all but the most persistent rain until cutting was completed and the slow process of carting and stacking could go on. In suitable weather and with plenty of labour, some sheaves might be taken and stacked straight from the field. At other times mows might be thrown open to dry and then be rebuilt several times before being fit to cart. In unrelenting bad weather, some corn would stand in the fields until the grains sprouted. This would be gradually carted throughout the winter and fed in the sheaf to housed animals. Even as late as December, in snow, hail or rain, this harvesting might continue, the frozen heads tinkling as they were moved.

The final stage would occur with the three or four threshing sessions that released the grain and completed the winter season. – *Ruth Barry*

## A year on The Ling

THAT year on the Ling at Garboldisham (pronounced Garblesham locally) in the early 1950s was like no other before or since. As recently as 1952 a mixed farm of 500 acres was still worked by 33 men only two of whom had long passed forty, and still employed ten working horses – all grey Percherons. Just two tractors were kept, and though these did most of the ploughing, the two horsemen were kept busy opening the furrows for the tractor drivers, and laying the tops. They even ploughed one field hard by the main road so that passers-by could see how

**The Ling, Garboldisham, 1951**

ploughing should be done.

In the cowshed, a large building with gangways each side, a feed store at one end between the gangways and the dairy at the other, were standings for 104 Ayrshires, 26 backed on to either side of each gangway. They spent the winter tied in their standings, apart from a two hour period each morning when they went out on to nearby meadow to eat sugar beet tops while the muck was cleaned out of the cowshed, and new bedding and feed put in. Apart from being warm and comfortable, before the days of universal dehorning, they were unable to damage each other with their wide spread of horns.

Later developments in housing were undoubtedly more economical with space, especially when dehorning became the fashion, but there has never been any substitute for a cowshed full of cows with all the doors shut at five o'clock on a freezing January morning. Six men looked after the cows. Five on duty and one off at any given time. The three 'senior' cowmen had all worked on

the farm from leaving school. The other three were 'floating population' which came and went at fairly frequent intervals as cowmen seemed to in those days, looking for that job to end all jobs that was never around the corner.

The two most recent arrivals started their day going round half the cows each with a bucket of warm water to clean any muck from their udders. By the time they had finished, the second and third by seniority who were on duty, would be going down one on each side of the first gangway, and each with four bucket milking units. These were stood between each pair of cows in turn until all had been milked, driven by a vacuum pump in the boiler house behind the dairy, the vacuum airline running down each side of each gangway in front of the cows, with a tap for a rubber hose to be connected at each pair of stalls.

Milk from each cow was emptied into a carrying bucket for the senior man to carry to the dairy, climb three steps and pour it into a receiving tank, from whence it ran down a water operated milk cooler. Cold water was forced up, inside the cooler, whilst warm milk ran down the outside.

The juniors then had to scurry round behind the milking machines, hand stripping any milk that the machines had left. All 104 cows had to be milked, the milk in churns and on to the churn stand – thirty or more ten gallon churns each day – by the time the churn lorry arrived at 7.30 am. Then came the mucking out, washing down, feeding, straw carting and littering, not just of the cowshed, but also the yards housing young stock, calf pens, bull pens – three bulls were kept and some of these were of very uncertain temperament.

There was an hour allocated for breakfast at 8.30 am and two hours for lunch from twelve until 2.00 pm – providing all the necessary work had been finished by that time. Evening finish was usually between 5 and 6 pm, though even during the winter, there could be an extra call out for, for instance, occasional grooming of the cows.

The summer was quite different. The cows were out to grass and only visited the cowshed for milking. Many were dried off at that time, as calving was usually done in autumn for maximum winter milk production. So, did the cowmen have an easy time? They then had the opportunity of augmenting their fixed cowmen's wages by joining all the other men on the farm at piecework hoeing of sugar beet. Almost all what might

---

### Laughing Stock

CATTLE and stock shows abounded in the rural villages of Norfolk between the wars, and many rivalries developed between farmers to see who could produce the fattest pig or most fertile bull. These contests had more than pride at stake, however, for the market value of a prize animal could keep a farming family well-provisioned for an entire year.

At one such show, in the late 1930s, a bigger crowd than usual gathered close to the town of North Walsham when it was reported that farmer Ted Julian had produced the best bull seen in those parts for many a generation. News such as this excited the strong farming community in which everyone had a strong interest in cattle, both aesthetic and financial.

On the Saturday afternoon, in the main marquee, a tense hush fell over the audience when the MC announced jocularly: 'Now for the main exhibit of the day – farmer Julian's enormous bull whose charms are bound to bring a twinkle to the eye of many a lovelorn Daisy or Buttercup.'

The tent flap opened and with great dignity in strode not a champion bull but the rural district council chairman in his chain of office. His VIP smile turned to an expression of horror when, instead of polite applause, he was greeted by howls of bawdy laughter. – *Carl Hughes*

be termed 'gang' work was done on piecework basis, whether hoeing beet, knocking, topping and carting them off, or hedging, with differential rates depending on the age of the hedge. Also, everybody had to muck in at haymaking and harvest.

There were eleven farm cottages on the Ling and one or two more down in the village. Several of them had up to half an acre of land attached. Each in turn would either borrow a plough team, or persuade the horseman to plough their patch for them. They would all crop the majority of their patch with either potatoes or sugar beet, and would hoe them in their spare time. When lifting time came, if the crop were beet, they could all chip in together, and the boss would lend them the farm lorry to take their load to the factory, the resulting cheque being divided between those taking part.

All the permanent workers belonged to the Union, but there was never any discontent voiced. The Union membership meant that they had access to proper negotiations over piecework rates.

A wood on the farm had been felled but all the tops were left in situ and the boss wanted to clear the site for cultivation. All the workers were told that they could have Bonny (the cowshed horse) in the summer evenings and Saturday and Sunday afternoons, and the rulley (a low sideless wagon with a full lock and end ladders) and could cart as much firewood home as they liked. All good, seasoned oak.

One of the cowmen was semi local. His father had a small farm nearby,

so, working very hard, he carted to his father's some 35 rulley loads of wood. Then he borrowed a sawbench, cut it all up – and sold it. Little imagination is needed to understand on which side of the fence he was left. – *Alec Bull*

---

## Food for free

YOU were lucky, so they said, to live on a farm in the depression. All that free milk and butter, eggs and ducks and hens for the taking. So said the townees.

What they conveniently forgot was that we needed our produce to sell: our 'free' milk and butter and eggs and fowl were converted into clothes and shoes, tea and sugar. But they were right in a way, the townees. There were always the fruits of the field to be had for free. This, for us children, who longed for ice cream and chocolate and bananas, was a mixed blessing. But, with three generations to support and eight mouths to feed, we knew we must take what we could get.

Most highly prized, at least by the grown ups, was fried puffballs. It was a toss-up whether finding one was worth the penny reward or whether being obliged to eat the nauseous thing, sliced and fried in lashings of dripping, outweighed the benefit.

Stinging nettles, too, were said to be an excellent source of iron, not unlike spinach in flavour. This was, in itself, no recommendation. It was a constant dilemma whether to conceal the loathsome puffball under the nettles or the revolting nettles under the

**Eight mouths to feed...**

puffball. Either way, you were always found out and then forced to finish both.

Another delicacy, eaten under sufferance by us young 'uns, was nettle pudding: chopped nettles mixed with cabbage and barley and fat-bacon and boiled for hours in a muslin cloth.

Much more to our liking were field mushrooms, picked on mellow misty mornings in autumn and rushed home to be sizzled in a little bacon fat. Although, even these were fraught with danger. Uncle Wilt (newly grown up and seasoned seafarer) never tired of telling us how your tongue would fall right out from the root if you ate so much as a sliver of toadstool. Since Uncle Wilt had been all the way to Morocco and back, he was a font of great wisdom. Mushrooms in our house were eaten with grave suspicion and enjoyed only in retrospect.

Spicy watercress was a favourite. Picked from the bubbling Brook Furlong in late summer, when it was older and more flavoursome, it was an excellent accompaniment to the trout we sometimes caught from the same waters.

In autumn, there were berries (tiny raspberries and sweet strawberries, blackberries and rowan) and nuts (walnut and hazel, sweet chestnut and beech) to be gathered from the hedgerow. Preserved or pickled according to their nature, both berry and nut lasted well into summer.

Herbs, too, abounded We had not yet, in the thirties, acquired a continental taste for garlic, which grew in profusion, but wild chives we liked and basil and balm and thyme. And parsley. Ever resourceful, Gran did not waste precious parsley on mere garnish, but fried it in great bunches and served it in dollops alongside fish, or likely as not, the dreaded puffball. – *Valerie Jones*

# How to Trace Your Family Tree

## St Catherine's House and Civil Registration

CIVIL registration began in 1837 in England and Wales and 1855 in Scotland. Since then it has been a requirement to register all births, marriages and deaths on a central register, and receive a certificate showing the recorded details. This register is held by the Government and the indexes are in a building which today is known as St Catherine's House. Here we are going to look at civil registration and how St Catherine's House plays its role.

### Introduction

Acts of Parliament of 1836 and 1837 set up a system of civil registration in England and Wales of births, marriages and deaths. In addition these acts introduced the option to marry at a registry office or certain consecrated buildings such as non-conformist chapels, and catholic churches. Scotland followed in 1855 with a more elaborate system.

In 1837, England and Wales was split into 27 numbered districts under the supervision of a Superintendent Registrar, and these are further divided into sub-districts. Every time a birth, marriage

or death occurs a certificate is issued and an entry is made into a book. Every three months copies are made and sent to the General Registrar in London. National Indexes have been compiled from these copies and are open for public access at St Catherine's House. They are colour coded: red for births; green for marriages and black for deaths; and each index book represents three months' records. Microfilm copies have been made of these indexes which now means that instead of making a trip to London the same information can be seen at Mormon Family History Centres, County Record Offices and some larger libraries.

The indexes were hand written until 1866, and since then have been printed or typed. They do not give you the full details of what is on the certificate and copy certificates still have to be obtained to confirm the individual is your ancestor. The copy certificates however are no longer issued from St Catherine's House in London but from The General Registry Office, Smedley Hydro, Trafalgar Road, Southport PR8 2HH, where information is available including searches which will be carried out on your behalf for a fee.

One other alternative to St Catherine's House is to use the local registry offices, in the area where the event originally took place. If you know the registry office, you can write direct to them and for a fee they will carry out a five year search around the date you provide and issue a certificate, or return your fee if no entry is found. Alternatively, if you live within reach of the relevant local registry office then you can visit and see the original books for a fee and get copy certificates at a much lower cost than going to London, or Southport. The indexes at a local registry office are not necessarily in a true alphabetic sense, but are pages containing names beginning with the same letter. There can be many indexes to go through, as indexes are created for each sub-district, each church and hospital within a sub-district. Each index typically covers a ten-year period. You can obtain details of the local registry office in the phone book listed under 'Registrar of Births, Deaths and Marriages'.

## St Catherine's House

St Catherine's House is a large building situated at 10 Kingsway, London WC2B 6JP. Held in this building are the indexes to those birth, marriage and death certificates that have been filed; Adoption Registers from 1927; Still Birth Registers since 1927; Marine Registers from 1837 covering births and deaths at sea; Air Registers covering births and deaths on aircraft since 1949; Armed Forces birth, marriage and death registers from about 1881 and other miscellaneous registers.

A trip to St Catherine's House will take you to a building situated on the corner of Kingsway and Aldwych and if going by tube the nearest stations are Holborn and Temple. They are open from 8.30am to 4.30pm Monday to Friday.

On entering the building you will see racks containing forms. These are colour coded as red for births, green for marriages and purple or mauve for deaths. You fill in the base details you already know and then consult the bookshelves. The bookshelves contain the quarterly indexes and from the spine you can identify which book you require. The date on the spine is the last month covered and the initial letters shown are the initial letters of the surnames covered in that volume. If you identify the person you think you are looking for then write down the full reference on to the form you picked up on entry and hand it into the desk with your fee. You can then arrange either to receive a copy of the original certificate by post or return to St Catherine's House to collect it several days later.

Birth indexes prior to July 1946 will give you the surname, first names, registration district, volume and page number of the original. However, since 1946 the mother's maiden name will also be shown. In the marriage indexes the certificate is indexed under both parties' names. Prior to 1912 you will get the full name of the person, the superintendent registrar's district and volume and page number of the original. Since 1912 you also have the addition of the surname of the spouse following the full name. The death indexes on the other hand have had three changes. Prior to 1866, just the name, superintendent registrar's district, volume and page number are given. From 1866 to 1969 you also have the addition of Age at Death (although this is often wrong); and from 1969 the Date of Birth of the deceased is given (again often wrong).

*A few points to watch out for when searching the indexes are:*
Double-barrelled names are indexed under the complete name ignoring the hyphen and are under the letter of the first part of the name; for example an entry for John Smith-Bailles will appear under S. The volume number on the spine is the number of the region incorporating the registration district.

Parents are allowed 42 days to register a birth, although most do not take this long. It does however mean that a February birth may not be in the index ending March and therefore it is wise to check the next quarter. If the parents were not married you will normally find the father's name omitted until recently. However since 1875 the father's name has been allowed to be included if he accompanied the mother to register and accepted paternity. In these cases the index entry will be both under the mother's and father's surname. Foundlings will usually be

recorded in the index after the letter Z.

Also watch out for mis-spellings or spelling variations. Some people within the same family are known to have spelt their names differently. Indexing errors are another problem, when copying from one source to another. For example a church wedding will be added originally into the church's book, then it will be copied on a form and sent to the local registry office where it is then copied into their index and another form is completed and forwarded to London, where somebody else then copies it into the index.

## Preparation and Tools

There are many books making up these indexes and browsing through them with no purpose will not be thrilling, enlightening or even a good use of your time, if you have travelled to London.

St Catherine's House is a busy place and you may not be able to get to that index you want straight away, so set yourself a target list of what you want to achieve. Before you set out on your journey identify from the information you have already collected which certificates you want to find. Create some forms like the ones for Birth/Marriage/Death Index Search, Birth/Marriage/Death Certificate Summary and St Catherine's House Index Check List before you leave. These will help ensure you collect all the information you can from the indexes, as well as identify those indexes to which you have not yet had access because others were using them.

| FHE15 | | BIRTHS/MARRIAGE/DEATH INDEX SEARCH | | | | | | |
|---|---|---|---|---|---|---|---|---|
| | | | KEY FAMILY: | | | | | |
| Year | Qtr | Name(s) | Mother's Name | Spouse | Age | Reg. District | Vol | Pg |
| | | | | | | | | |

Variants on spelling:

Search Carried Out At:      Date:

## Birth/Marriage/Death Index Search

When searching the indexes at St Catherine's House, each year is split into quarter indexes. Therefore there are a lot of indexes to go through. This form allows you to record those individuals' details which interest you, from the index and reference, so you can refer back or obtain the certificates. Each form is based on a family surname.

## Birth/Marriage/ Death Certificate Summary

This form you may not find as useful at St Catherine's House as you would if you went along to a local registry office and were able to look at the original record. You will find it useful when visiting relations and

---

| FHE4 | | | | BIRTH/MARRIAGE/DEATH CERTIFICATE SUMMARY | | | | | | |
|---|---|---|---|---|---|---|---|---|---|---|
| | | | | | KEY FAMILY: | | | | | |

Registration District: _____ App No: _____

Date: _____ BIRTH in sub-district of _____

_____ in the _____

| NO | when & where | Name | Sex | Father | Mother | Father Occup. | Signature and Residence | Sig of Reg |
|---|---|---|---|---|---|---|---|---|
| | | | | | | | | |

Superintendant Registrar    Date:

Registration District: _____ App No: _____

Date: _____ MARRIAGE solemnized at _____

in the parish of _____ in the _____

| No | when | Name(s) | Age | Status | Occup. | Residence | Father | Occup. |
|---|---|---|---|---|---|---|---|---|
| | | | | | | | | |

Married in the _____ according to the _____ of the

The marriage solemnized by us _____ in the presence of _____

Registration District: _____ App No: _____

Date: _____ DEATH in sub-district of _____

_____ in the _____

| No | when & where | Name | Sex | Age | Occup. | Cause of Death | Res. of Inf. | when Reg. | Sig Reg. |
|---|---|---|---|---|---|---|---|---|---|
| | | | | | | | | | |

---

| FHE22 | St Catherine's House Index Check List |
|---|---|

Type of Index (i.e. Birth, Marriage, Death): _____ Colour: _____

Date Of Visit: _____ Key Family: _____

☐ Not Applicable    ☑ Entry Found    ☒ No Entry

| Year | | | | | | | | | | | | | | | | |
|---|---|---|---|---|---|---|---|---|---|---|---|---|---|---|---|---|
| Names | 1 | 2 | 3 | 4 | 1 | 2 | 3 | 4 | 1 | 2 | 3 | 4 | 1 | 2 | 3 | 4 |
| | | | | | | | | | | | | | | | | |

| Year | | | | | | | | | | | | | | | | |
|---|---|---|---|---|---|---|---|---|---|---|---|---|---|---|---|---|
| Names | 1 | 2 | 3 | 4 | 1 | 2 | 3 | 4 | 1 | 2 | 3 | 4 | 1 | 2 | 3 | 4 |
| | | | | | | | | | | | | | | | | |

| Year | | | | | | | | | | | | | | | | |
|---|---|---|---|---|---|---|---|---|---|---|---|---|---|---|---|---|
| Names | 1 | 2 | 3 | 4 | 1 | 2 | 3 | 4 | 1 | 2 | 3 | 4 | 1 | 2 | 3 | 4 |
| | | | | | | | | | | | | | | | | |

*The design of the certificates is Crown copyright and is reproduced with the permission of the controller HMSO*

you are unable to take a copy of the original certificate. If you have the original, entering the details on this form will mean you will cut down the wear and tear on the original.

## St Catherine's House Index Check List

This form will allow you to keep track of those index volumes you have already managed to see or the ones which interest you. If you head the form with the date of your visit and make a note of those you are interested in and mark up those you managed to see, those you did not manage to see can be transferred to another form when you return home, ready for your next visit. You can adapt this also to cover those index searches you may carry out at local registry offices.

## The Certificates

When you have done your search of the indexes you will request copies of the certificates. Research you

have carried out in the marriage and death certificates and other sources will have already ensured that you have the right individual. Getting the birth certificate will only confirm this.

## Birth Certificates

Since 1 July 1837 any parent registering a birth of their child has in return received a certificate showing the details which have been recorded. Up until 1875 when compulsory registration came into effect not all births were registered. The certificate carries the following information; on the top, the details of the registration district which is usually a large town, the sub-district name and county together with year of birth. On the bottom, the date when registered; the signature of the registrar and the registrar's full name. In the middle of the certificate the layout is in columns and information is shown in the following order: number (this is the entry number in the register); when and where born (if a time is stated it usually indicates a multiple birth, although in some areas registrars recorded the time on all certificates); name of child (if any); sex; name and surname of father (if left blank usually indicates an unmarried mother); name, surname and maiden name of mother; occupation of father; and finally the signature, description and residence of the informant.

### Marriage Certificates

1837 saw the introduction of marriages at registry offices and other consecrated venues other than just the Church of England. Since this time, an entry is made in a register and a certificate issued to the couple showing those details recorded and proving the event took place.

When you obtain a copy certificate from the registrar it will give you the following details. It starts off by giving the registration district and the wording of 'Marriage solemnised at XY in the parish of [name of parish] in the county of [name of county]; followed by nine columns of which the first is the entry number in the register; the date of the marriage; name and surname of couple with their ages (often wrong, sometimes shown as 'of full age', 'over 21' all meaning 21 or over), status, profession and residence at time of marriage (sometimes entered as the same address to avoid banns having to be called in both parishes); the names of the fathers and their occupations. It is then finished off with the signatures of the married couple, their witnesses (usually

other members of the family or friends) and that of the person carrying out the marriage.

### Death Certificates

The death certificate gives the following information; the details of the registration district, sub district and county; the year and entry number in the register; when and where the person died; name and surname; sex; age; occupation; cause of death; signature and residence of the informant; when registered and the signature of the registrar.

After 1 April 1969 a few minor changes occurred: the date of birth instead of age of the deceased is shown; the deceased's maiden name is shown if a married woman; details of usual residence and place of birth are also itemised.

### Conclusion

If you use the St Catherine's House route with postal searches and trips to London, you will find this can become expensive and the waiting period makes the whole process a little slow.

There are faster and much less expensive alternatives to consider. One of these for obtaining a marriage certificate might be to use a microfilm copy of the St Catherine's House index to find the marriage, identify when it took place and make a note of the registration district. Visit the registry office and use the marriage index to find the church where the marriage took place and then visit the relevant county record office to see the church register and copy out the details.

# Badge of Pride

**WESLEY HARRY (lately Historian, The Royal Arsenal, Woolwich) writes:**

I recently received the first and second issues of *Country Origins* (I was so pleased with my membership copy number three, that I felt I must have the earlier issues!).

I was interested in the article entitled 'Black Powder', and especially the photograph of two female workers. (*Country Origins*, Autumn 1995, page 125) I think I can date the pictures to 1916. These triangular, brass badges were issued as a means of indicating that

the date 1918, but most are of 1916, when many women were entering the war effort in order to release able young men for the services.

War workers were proud to wear these badges, and you will find many photographs of workers in their pro-

tective clothing, displaying their badge.

Workers were also issued with certificates indicating that the person named was employed on war work.

At the end of hostilities the certificate was to be returned to the War Office, and, provided every month in which the holder had been employed was stamped or initialled, a medal would be issued. (A promise quietly forgotten after the war!)

the wearer was in fact playing his/her part in the war effort, and hopefully would prevent men, especially, being given the white feather.

I have seen a few badges bearing

# Book Reviews

### The Women's Land Army and Me
Marjorie M Dean.
143 x 210 132 pages
Some black and white photographs
Published by
The Pentland Press Ltd
ISBN 1–85821–311–8 Paperback
£8.50

MARJORIE DEAN the author served her country during World War 2 by being part of the 90,000 strong Women's Land Army. The Land Army played an important role during the Second World War by allowing able-bodied farm workers to go in the Armed services and by increasing home food production. Every member who took part was a volunteer. Much of the work carried out by the farm labourer was done by hand, and most farms still used horses – very few had tractors. A Land Girl was expected to take on such tasks as dairy food production, horticulture and animal husbandry. This book takes you on a journey through the author's eyes from the day she left her post office job in London, to arriving in North Tawton in Devon for her new job.

She then takes you through her daily life in rural Devon and the work of the Land Army together with the new friends she made, the heavy farm work they had to do, their fears, and their loves. Although emigrating to Australia in 1960 she was able to keep in touch with some of the new friends she made, and the book goes right through to a reunion that took place in 1994 when Marjorie and her husband returned to England for a five month holiday. The book is a compelling read and the little anecdotes such as that of the knicker elastic puts a smile on your face.

### Discovering Horse Brasses
John Vince.
114 x 177 48 pages
Centre 16 pages containing black and white photographs of many brass designs
Published by Shire Publications
ISBN 0–85263–014-X Paperback
£2.75

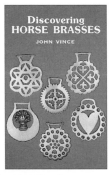

THE history of the horse brass seems to come from old folklore where it was believed that the sun and moon had an impact on the environment around us, and these elements would determine whether or not the harvest would be a fruitful one. One primary feature of all primitive societies is the preoccupation with the evil eye, and its relation to catastrophe. The horse and the ox pulled the ploughs through the fields previously and for thousands of years were an important part of power and needed protection. Some of the earliest amulets found back to the fifth millennium BC were simple discs marked with sunlike rays.

The age of chivalry also adds some insight to the idea that discs and decoration had some role to play as they had no functional purpose. For instance in the case of the horses used in the joust and on the battlefield, although clothed heavily in armour they would also be decorated with plumes.

Very few horse brasses exist prior to the 19th century, possibly because they were melted down during Queen Victoria's reign. Very little written evidence exists to explain why they were created and why so many designs, but knowing what we do about folklore and people's beliefs would indicate that these brasses had a more important role than just decoration.

This little pocket sized book looks at the origins of the brasses, how the horse played a very important role in farming communities and in the transport provision of this country. The text then explains how the brasses are manufactured and tries to interpret some of the many hundreds of designs and their significance using pictures.

**How It All Began**
*The stories behind those famous names*

Maurice Baren.
239 x 228 126 pages Many black and white and colour photographs and illustrations
Published by Smith Settle Ltd
ISBN 1–870071–92–1 Paperback
£8.95

A GOOD coffee table book which you can pick up and put down as you want and still glean more information about the history behind those well known brand names. Those everyday products we take for granted come to life with the brief descriptions of their history and how they came about. For example Pears Soap was an invention of Andrew Pears who was the son of a Cornish Farmer in Mevagissey and trained as a hairdresser. Once trained he moved to London and manufactured rouges, creams, powders and other beauty aids in his hairdressers' shop. His translucent and slightly perfumed soap became popular for being less harsh on the skin than others of the time and a manufacturing process took hold and grew. Also did you know that Marmite was the result of fermentation of yeast used for making beer? The Oxford dictionary defines Marmite as being 'an extract from fresh brewers yeast, rich in Vitamin B complex. Used for culinary purposes and also medicinally'.

**Till Death Us Do Part – A Vet's Life**
Richard Holden.
160 x 240 242 pages
Published by The Pentland Press ISBN 1–85821–240–5 Hardback £14.95

THE author being a country vet has written a story but based on facts and his own experiences of the time. The story opens in the winter of 1942 with a farmer's son reporting that a cow they had bought that day had fallen into a tank and they required help to retrieve it. He dresses in his old clothes and leaves for the remote farm in the cold snowy weather. Communications in Lancashire back in 1942 and of course during the war were not as good as they are today – no mobile phone could be put in the pocket! So on leaving the house he asked his wife to pass on any messages of other help required in that area to the local post office and he would call in there on the way back. He uses the relevant dialogue and portrays a picture of country life still on the move although the country was at war. The use of the dialogue can be a little tricky for someone not from Lancashire, but don't let this put you off – it is a good read. It shows his practice getting busier daily and how he continues on his daily rounds of difficult calvings, milk fever, mastitis and wooden tongue. The characters he meets come to life and are full of colour, some being more helpful than others. At times the book is amusing, frequently tragic and totally engaging. It gives a fascinating insight into the daily life of a country professional in rural England during the war.

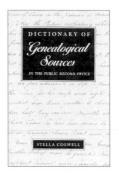

**Dictionary of Genealogical Sources**
*In the Public Record Office*
Stella Colwell.
160 x 240 206 pages.
Published by George Weidenfeld & Nicholson Ltd
ISBN 0–297–83140–2. Hardback £20.00

THE sub-title on this book is important. It is laid out like a dictionary, entries are in alphabetical order with descriptions and details of the records that can be found at the Public Record Office. It has tried to organise it a topic at a time and at the end of an item in nearly all cases it will give cross references of other sections to look under. However, you do have to be aware of what it is you are looking for and what all the possibilities and combinations could be, to make sure you have identified everything possible. Before you start, sit down with a piece of paper and write down all the possible connections with a subject, then you stand a better chance of finding what you are looking for. For example looking up 'education' will result in a blank, but think of school teachers, schools, poor law unions, and so on, and your search will be fruitful. You will identify some of the records at the PRO relating to this topic – by no means all, but you have to start somewhere.

## The County Maps of Old England *as drawn by Thomas Moule*

Introduced by Roderick Barron.
264 x 364 128 pages
56 coloured maps
Published by Studio Editions Ltd
ISBN 1–85170–403–5 Hardback
£9.95

THOMAS Moule was a Victorian map maker. First published in 1830 they portray an England where old values could still be found. At the time of compiling them history was still alive in country houses, parish churches, market towns and places and country scenes. This book has put together those maps which first appeared between 1842 and 1853 together with 19th century descriptions of the counties and details of their main towns. The book starts with a small introduction written by Roderick Barron on the cartographer Thomas Moule himself, his thoughts of the time and how the maps were made. The write up on the county gives details of its position in relation to other counties of England, some idea of population, town size and such little things as how many MPs at the time it sent to London. A treasure trove of information. The maps are splendid, beautifully colourful, and detailed enough to show names of places in the English of the day, railway lines, rivers and roads.

## The Family Tree Detective

Colin D Rogers.
138 x 215 182 pages
Published by Manchester University Press
ISBN 0–7190–1846–3
Paperback £7.95

FOR a Family History book this one is a little unusual in that rather than repeating the same information as many of the others and taking the author's family as an example, this one looks at the problems you may come across whilst doing your research and how to overcome them. Its sub-title is 'a manual for analysing and solving genealogical problems in England and Wales 1538 to the present day'. It looks primarily at the five main sources of records we delve into on the start of our research of births, deaths, and marriages, the censuses and wills. It points you in other directions and to other sources that you may not first think of when you hit a problem. The appendices at the end give some useful addresses and places you can look for.

# Countryside Classics

THE Rev. J.G. Wood, MA., FLS. was the name beneath the title of an old book on the second-hand bookshop shelf. *Out of Doors*, 1890, Longmans, Green & Co., London, New Edition said the flyleaf and inside was scrawled a signature and 1891, the signing of a former owner. 105 years ago someone had written his name and the date 4th November in this little treasure which now stands on a shelf in my study with its foxing and pressed bramble leaf, found between pages 192 and 193 where there is also a detailed picture captioned 'My Blackberry Tree'. I felt somehow the leaf and the 1891 owner were linked and will not part with it. Old books have their stories beyond that of the text, mysteries of previous owners we can but guess at.

But J.G. Wood will go down in natural history as one of the best known of country writers, his books those pleasant rambles through the countryside that not only teach us so much on the way but are in a style that paints pictures with words. All too rare these days.

Others of his works to seek include

**Goldfinch at nest – one of the creatures discussed by J.G. Wood in his classic...**
*Our Garden Friends and Foes*

*Homes Without Hands, Insects At Home, The Handy Natural History, Strange Dwellings, Petland Revisited* and *Bible Animals*, the latter a description of every living creature mentioned in the scriptures, with 122 illustrations.

Indeed the illustrations were a keynote of his books, beautifully detailed and by various artists. I particularly love those in *A Brook And Its Banks*, a delightful tale with some fine artwork which gels perfectly with the text in this one of the author's last books and published by The Religious Tract Society.

Readers of Wood will have to realise that like many writers of his day, quite a number of them churchmen, he often shot the very creatures he wrote about, this in the days of the old ball-shot weapons. It seems best to refer to it here as Wood refers to it a few times himself but do not be deterred, here is a fine author with a deserved reputation for his style, his personal experience in the field and that lovely way of imparting to the reader his many fascinating observations of the countryside. – *Trevor Beer*

# Clatter of the Iron Road

## *Fred Archer*

IT was a very similar situation planning the Little Branch Railway Line from Ashchurch to Barnt Green as occurs today when a bypass road is built for motor vehicles.

The branch line left the main railway as Ashchurch going along the Carrant Valley and the Avon Valley to connect again with the main line at Barnt Green.

The route originally planned passed through a little farm owned by Mrs Abel. A grasping solicitor bought this little farm by taking from a Mr Baldwyn the Deeds of his house and using the £6,000 for the purchase of the farm. The railway company altered the route to avoid the flooding of Mrs Abel's farm. The solicitor was jailed for fraud after going bankrupt. Mr Baldwyn lost his £6,000.

The railway company planned their line to go through Joseph New's farm at Ashton under Hill but said there would not be a railway station there. Mr New said:

'If you don't make a station at Ashton under Hill you are not coming through my farm.' It appears that in that year of 1864 land owners were not threatened with Compulsory Purchase.

A station was built and Mr New's neighbours, including Squire Baldwyn, presented him with a Silver Cup for his efforts to get a station in the village. The opening of the railway line was celebrated with a village show and feast, organised by Squire Baldwyn.

With the new branch line, excursions from the village station took folk to the city and the sea-side. So many had never seen the sea or even been to Birmingham or Bristol.

From the railway station at Ashton parties of villagers went via Ashchurch to Sharpness on the River Severn where they boarded a steamer down the Bristol Channel to Ilfracombe. The liberation the railway brought to village folk was amazing. In 1890 a party from the village station took a train to Southampton and a steamer to Cherbourg.

There were problems for the farm workers who visited the sidings loading produce for the city markets. The

**Little Tank Engine similar to the one which pulled the Pick Up on the branch line**

*Above top*: **A passenger train in Ashton under Hill Station. Note the double track on the permanent way. This engine would push or pull the carriages from Ashchurch to Birmingham via Barnt Green.**
*Above*: **After Beeching's axe of the line of 1964 and the tracks ripped up. The fire buckets are still hanging on the wall by the Waiting Room. The house in the background is where the Porter in Charge lived.**

horses pulling the carts and waggons had not experienced the hissing of steam and the clouds of smoke from railway engines. Canny farmers owning the land beside the line grazed their horses in the fields so that they became used to the clatter of trains on the iron road.

Before the railway came the market gardeners and fruit growers of the Vale under Bredon Hill marketed

their produce in the local markets. The railway siding now became full of a line of trucks and goods vans which took the produce to points North – Liverpool; Manchester; Nottingham; Newcastle and so on.

The Company, everyone called it the Company, made a ruling that each consignment of fruit and vegetables was charged for half a ton weight. The Little Master Men of the day cooperated together to make up the 10 cwt load by pooling their produce.

Every afternoon at 3.30 a little tank engine took the trucks and vans of produce to Evesham. The engine, known as The Pick Up, finished its journey from the village sidings at a marshalling yard there where the goods trains were organised for distant markets. As the M1 was a novelty when it first opened so these railway lines often caused humour among the new travelling public.

'How long will the train be, Porter?' Squire Baldwyn asked a hopeful in his sleeved waistcoat.

Ray thought a while then replied, 'Not quite as long as the platform, Sir.'

Jonathan, a village carpenter, took the train home one evening from where he had been working.

'Tickets, please!' the porter shouted.

'Not mine, you won't. I paid for that bit of pasteboard.'

The station at Ashton was manned by a Porter in Charge, a sandy-haired, sandy-moustached chap known as a Company's Man. He refused to strike when other men downed tools. His office was loud with the sound of the telegraph machine which he decoded only when the message was for his station.

It was always warm in the Booking Office and George, the Porter in Charge, was loath to leave that comfortable room in winter. If Ray was not around, George's job was to accompany the men with the produce, open the doors of the goods van and count the number of hampers and check with the consignment note.

'I'm busy,' he often said. 'You can manage, the van for Nottingham is already open, give me the consignment note.' Bert the drayman was not pleased, threatening to report George to Derby. He never did.

Horses and dray were continually travelling up and down the Groaten, which became known as Station Road. Loads of cattle cake in slabs from Gloucester all came to the siding. The service was so good that produce loaded at the station in the afternoon arrived at the markets in the north early next morning. If fog or disruption made the train miss the market George issued Claim Forms.

Milk went from the station in 17 gallon churns to Birmingham. To see George or Ray bowling those tall churns when they were empty was a picture. They bowled them along the station platform two at a time.

In the station yard Billy Drinkwater had a Coal Wharf where he weighed the coal from a truck into one hundredweight sacks. Billy's horse and dray delivered coal around the villages. If the truck of coal was not unloaded within a certain time Billy had to pay the company demurrage. Loads of coal to the big houses

were delivered in dray loads after being weighed at the weigh bridge.

In this age of speed and looking back to the branch line which ran for nearly one hundred years until it was axed by Beeching, one wonders. The journey of 36 miles to Birmingham took one and a half hours stopping at around twenty stations, but the 7.20 am train did arrive in the middle of the city – no traffic jams.

Some railways have been opened by enthusiasts. During the war the branch line took traffic off the main line to leave it clear for munitions and such, but the Banana Train never chuffs through the night air on its way from Avonmouth to Birmingham these days. The labouring noise it made sounded painful as its load of fruit taxed the engine up the Stanborough Incline. Now there is nostalgia about the steam trains which are no more. Perhaps they weren't appreciated in their day. Men in the fields set their watches by them in the days before the wireless.

**17-gallon milk churns, like the ones which the porters rolled along the platform two at a time**

# The Walter Rose Collection

## A window on yesterday's world

THIS story begins in 1857. Queen Victoria had been on the throne for twenty years, the Great Exhibition in Hyde Park had been and gone, a Peace Treaty had been signed in Paris ending the Crimean War and Walter Rose was born. The birth of a baby son to an agricultural labourer in a small Surrey village was not destined to make much of an impression upon the record books, but possibly

**A fine pair of dappled grey shires are pulling a cart belonging to Kent & Chalke of Milton Farm, Westacott, Surrey, noted as one of the last farms in the area to grow, harvest and distil peppermint**

his real worth has remained hidden until now.

John and Jane Rose raised the young Walter and his siblings, Ernest and Amos in Westcott near Dorking, sending them to the village school where Walter was to see the Headmaster, Charles Brown, experimenting with the new art-form of photography. The wet-collodion process, where the user had to coat his glass-plates with light-sensitive 'emulsion' before use, was still firmly established and was not to be ousted until the 1870s, with the introduction of gelatin dry plates.

Walter was not able to follow a

career in photography upon leaving school, for it was chiefly a fashionable pastime for the leisured and wealthy classes, so he entered service in a large house on Westcott Common called Holcombe, alongside his brother Ernest who was already employed there as a gardener.

He attempted to better himself

**On the left stands John Rose, father of Walter and on the right is a young man whom Dolly Rose could only ever remember being called 'that boy-chap'**

and applied for a position in the library at Harrow School upon the advice of the art teacher William Egerton Hine, a friend of the Roses

A hopsaver in Deerleap Woods on the North Downs in Surrey. He would have been one of the many itinerant workers making their living from managing the woodland. The hoops, stacked to the left of the shelter, were used in the making of barrels and cases, with the largest and longest hoops going to the West Indies for sugar hogsheads.

and a Westcott resident. This proved to be unsuccessful and Walter chose to try to make a living out of photography.

Now married to Ellen, they converted the shed in the garden of the small house in Westcott Street into a darkroom and erected a wooden studio in the front garden.

The principal source of income would have derived from family portraiture, commissions from wealthy landowners and the printing of picture postcards, which were sweeping the nation by the early 20th century as a collecting craze, sustaining many

a small-time village photographer.

Walter and Ellen had no children, but raised their niece Dolly, whose mother had died on the day that she was born. Walter clearly doted on this young girl and took many charming photographs of her, usually surrounded by her collection of wooden toys or the family pets. As she grew older, Dolly was often called upon to help Uncle Walter process his plates and then make prints from them.

The business struggled on until the 1920s, by which time Walter had reached retirement age and thereafter he only took the occasional photograph, consigning his collection of glass-plate negatives to the garden shed darkroom, where they were to remain for he next forty years. Ellen Rose died in 1935 leaving Dolly to look after Walter until his death in 1954 at the age of 97.

During the 1960s, a young Westcott man, David Knight, was

*Above*: A charming study of a boy and his donkey. What was he carrying in the panniers?
*Below*: A picture taken on Dolly's fourth birthday. Some of the toys may have been gifts whilst others may have been passed on by her older sister 'Nell'.

**Ellen 'Nell' Rose, niece of Walter, posing for a portrait with a very tame chicken**

busy compiling his own archive of local history and it was to him that Dolly Rose turned when she was seeking a good home for her uncle's invaluable pictorial record of the area in the form of 900 glass-plate negatives, lantern slides and photographic prints.

Before his untimely death in 1995, David Knight allowed the Dorking photographer Keith Harding complete access to his 'treasure trove' and

*Above*: The village school in Westcott provided Walter Rose with more than just his education, for it was the headmaster Charles Brown who first introduced him to the art of photography. The pupils depicted here are attending a life-drawing class with their hands clasped firmly behind their backs in the belief that it would discourage any of them from becoming left-handed.

*Below*: Miss 'Becky' Greathurst, an assistant teacher at Westcott school between 1879 and 1925, demonstrates the art of forming letters, whilst the junior pupils trace the characters with their forefingers in sand trays

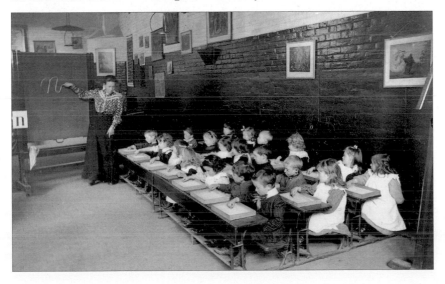

*Above*: Aberconwy, Wales c1890
*Below*: Harrow-on-the-hill, famous for its public school has seen little change since this photograph was taken around 1890. Walter Rose applied for a job in the library at Harrow School and may have taken this view at that time.

once this had been removed to his studio Harding began the painstaking task of proof-printing every item for identification and cataloguing. Now that this task has been completed, copies of Walter Rose's photographs are once again available for purchase with the rare distinction of having been printed directly from the original glass negatives.

Hand-printed photographs from Walter Rose's negatives can be obtained from Keith Harding, Goodness Gracious, Jayes Park Courtyard, Lake Road, Ockley, Surrey, RH5 5RR. Tel: 01306 621474 for further details.

A selection of those photographs taken locally appear in *Dorking and district old photographs, from Walter Rose Collection*. Alan Sutton Publishing Ltd. ISBN 0 7509 0550 6

*Above*: A regular sight in the Surrey market town of Dorking was the circus parade. In this photograph, Lord George Sanger's circus is making its way from the railway station to the public space known as the Cotmandene which played host to public events and is still home for visiting fun-fairs.

*Below*: A gypsy with his 'dancing' bear in Dorking High Street, Surrey, must have been a strange sight to untravelled and mostly unread village people

## REFLECTIONS

# Fruit Picking and Field Work in East Kent

IN Summer *Country Origins*, Olive Tumber talked to Jacqueline Sarsby about her childhood. *After she had left school, Olive Tumber had several jobs in service. At first she was scrubbing floors in a hotel, (where she was so home-sick for her mother, she caught the train home and never went back), then she worked in a shop, and afterwards, looked after a farmer's children – each time, for different reasons, wanting to come home. Eventualy she went home to look after the family, because her mother was seriously ill. She worked in the fields during the day to earn money,* '… Pulling swedes and shocking corn, sort of doing anything so you could get some money…' *Her father was earning little more, but he had the considerable expense of doctor's bills.*

*Swede-pulling was a cold, November job, working out in the field on her own with a little spotty dog for company. She would have 'a cant', about a quarter of an acre, to work, pulling out the swedes of about a dozen rows, ringing off their leaves and putting them in piles up the field, then covering them with the leaves, so that* they would not get frosted overnight. *She remembered two school-boys, who used to come and spend Saturdays earning a little pocket-money, when the young corn was growing, bird-scaring with wooden clappers and a gun – they would make a fire, put on a tin kettle and make tea. She had happy memories of field work,* '… I like the open-air life – I'm much better out in the open air, that's why I like being out in the fields: we've been picking sprouts with snow on them and ice – never had a cold, truthfuly, never had a cold…!'

*Later on, she worked with a thrashing machine:* '… The first time I was behind the thrashing machine, that was at Ash, and they wanted someone to feed the engine with water – so [*the farmer*] came and asked me if I would go and do it. I had a yoke on my shoulders with chains and buckets. I used to go to the tap and get the water, and put it in this huge tank in the engine. Of course, it overflowed – I worked too hard! Oh they did pull my leg!…' *On another farm, she and three other women raked up the chaff, as it came out of the thrashing machine, and bagged it up, to be scattered in the cattle yards.*

*She also pulled leeks and packed them for market, chopped worzels and bagged them up for the calves to eat. She continued working outdoors after she was married, doing all the different jobs according to the season. In the Spring there was hop-training, which was 'twiddling' the young hop-bines (or stems) up strings or poles, and tying them in with wet rushes. Hop-bines break easily:* '… The hop-bine is a little bit prickly and very very brittle… You've got to be very careful…' *Hop-training went on for about three months until the hop-bines took off up the strings on their own,* '… You keep on at it until the farmer says, "Oh, they're firing away now, no need to do any more!"…'

*After hop-training came fruit -picking:* '… I used to start, say, when the strawberries started – that was in June – we used to work right through till November. That was with apples and plums and pears, and then ended up with tree-banding – put the bands round the trees, then put the sticky stuff on with a brush so that the insects don't get up in the tree…'

*Strawberry-picking involved an early start:* '… I used to leave the children with my husband, I used to go with the eldest, 3 o'clock in the morning, strawberry-picking and then – I used to have my bike – we'd get back home about half past six, then I'd got to pack my husband's sandwiches, cook his breakfast, get the children up and dressed and get down there again for 7 o'clock, and go on until 12. Then 12 till 1, sit down, have a rest and have your dinner

(well, we called it lunch, whatever) and then you worked till 5 o'clock. then get home and get on with it – you wouldn't get your jobs done otherwise!… We had to be down picking strawberries at 3 o'clock, because the birds would get out and eat them. That was the best time to pick them – keep the birds off…'

*She used to go cherry-picking at Bramling, taking her baby in her 'old working pram', and enjoying the company:* '… When we were cherry-picking, there used to be one woman in particular, she used to make a camp-fire and make tea, and we'd all sit round having cups of tea, when it was our break-time…'

*All sorts of people used to go cherry-picking:* '… We used to meet up in

**Olive Tumber in the cherry orchard, cherry-picking in the 1930s**

(Photo from J. Sarsby)

the orchard. We had some lovely times up there – even the mayoress of Sandwich used to come out cherry picking – lots of titled ladies we had up there! We had a marvellous time! You'd get up a ladder, you have a basket with a hook on it. You hook that on to a bough, and then you've got your hands free, (you've got to know the ropes, standing on a ladder – one woman fell off) and if you hook your basket on the tree, you hang on with one hand and you can pick your fruit down into your basket. I used to love it…!'

*Pickers were divided into two groups, the home-pickers, who lived locally, and the outsiders (from Canterbury or Adisham), each with their own ladderman, who would move and secure the ladders in the trees, and decide when to move on. They were big trees, and three people and their ladders might be picking at the same time in one tree.*

*Cherry-picking did not mean such an early start, so she could do overtime in the evening: '… I worked all day up till 5 o'clock, and then sometimes I've* gone home and cooked a dinner, like a main meal, and done some washing, then gone back again and worked for 7 o'clock, cherry-picking… I enjoyed it, and I wanted the money, to get clothes for the children, and I just loved it. You get nice company. You're shut in if you're at home – well, I used to go out with the babies, when I wasn't working, I really enjoyed it…

'… It was lovely up at 6 in the morning. I loved it. I used to get up and get my work done, get my washing done and out if it was nice, and I used to cook every other night – I'd get the veg and all ready – do you know, sometimes I think, well, how did I do it? Well, I did it. You've got to get up in the morning though – it's no good laying in bed and thinking what you've got to do. You've just got to get up and get on with it…!'

*Olive Tumber talked about her life to Dr Jacqueline Sarsby of the Countryside and Community Research Unit, Cheltenham and Gloucester College*

---

### R.A. King of Great Yarmouth writes:

You photo quoted as being Norwich market (page 86, Summer *Country Origins*) is quite wrong, it is Great Yarmouth market. The church above is the same as in the photo, minus steeple which was destroyed in the Second World War. The church was restored but not the steeple. I trust suitable retraction is made in the next edition of your excellent magazine.

*Thank you for correcting us. Collections of old photographs from all over the British Isles are often acquired complete with captions identifying the locations. Sadly, these are not always accurate but unless the collector is familiar with all the places in the photographs, it can be very difficult to verify each one. Your help will enable Mr Hannavy to amend his records. Many thanks. – Ed.*

# A Rhum Venture

*Rosalind Jones*

DONALD Cameron is a well loved personality of Fort William. His strict childhood, a lifetime of farming and auctioneering around Lochaber, the incomparable characters he met, and adventures experienced since the beginning of the century are captured in his book *While the Wild Geese Fly*. Meeting him not far from beautiful Glen Nevis that he once farmed, Donald opened windows on the past. One story he tells concerns his own unique contribution to the World War 2 effort.

'During the war, I was elected to be a representative for Lochaber for the Inverness-shire Agricultural Executive Committee. Attending a meeting one day the question was raised about the island of Rhum in relation to the war effort. "We haven't had an enquiry, far less an offer for the isle," the chairman told us. Whilst all the problems of tenanting the island were being discussed I was busy daydreaming about stories told me in my childhood by an old shepherd from Rhum, where wedder lambs weighed 80lbs and stags 18 stone. As a child I'd climbed Lochaber's mountains and looked over to Rhum's conical peaks wondering at its "magical" quality. Then suddenly I awoke from my dream when I realised I was being asked a question. "What do *you* propose we do, Cameron?" the chairman said. "I'll give you £50 a year for it!" I replied, joking. I only earned £6 a week at that time and I didn't have much money saved, but the chairman thought I was serious. "You've got it then!" he said. What *had* I let myself in for?'

Handed this unexpected challenge Donald scraped together some money and was determined to make a success of it. Anxious to see the 'magical' isle he drove northwest to Mallaig and caught the 'Lochmore' one of the small ferries that plied between the Hebridean islands. The ferry route to North and South Uist took in the small isles of Eigg, Rhum and Canna. On arrival he encountered the first in a series of handicaps that threatened to turn his venture into nothing but a 'rum deal'.

'The first problem I encountered was that the berth by Rhum's pier was silted up. The Lochmore offloaded me instead on to a small boat kept by the island's absentee lady owner. I realised immediately that this was going to be extremely difficult when offloading stock. Then I was met by the owner's head stalker who showed me around and introduced me to the fifteen inhabitants. He made it quite clear that the "laird"

the sheep fanks were dilapidated and dipping facilities were non-existent.'

Any level headed farmer would have backed out at this stage, but not Donald.

'It was my first financial venture and I was determined to succeed, so I signed for seven years at the £50 annual rent.'

With stipulations that his sheep stock was not to exceed 1,000 and his cattle 100, houses were made available for himself and shepherds, whilst a share of the steadings and two fields, one for hay, and one for handling the sheep and rams were allotted. Thinking that as Rhum had been cleared of sheep for twenty years there would be none of the common sheep diseases, and that as the isle was so windswept there would be no problem with maggot fly, he engaged a shepherd and in the autumn spent all his savings buying 600 blackface sheep. With no foxes on the island he reckoned he'd suffer no losses from predation.

'I dipped and dosed them and then accompanied them to Mallaig where we all boarded the *Lochmore*. The crew were none too pleased about me bringing along this smelly troublesome cargo. The sheep were problem enough to offload, but when it came to the small van I'd brought with me which had to be conveyed ashore via planks supported by the estate launch's gunnels it cost me a bottle of whisky and some rather fretful moments.'

Donald had planned that the sheep should be confined on the west side of Rhum, but as he still had to continue his work in Lochaber in his absence

**Donald Cameron at the sheep fank in Glen Nevis enjoying a cup of tea after shearing**

was not at all pleased that her private domain was to become part of the war effort to raise home produced meat, when for the previous twenty years it had been reserved for her private pleasure as a hunting estate!'

Guided around the mountainous lozenge-shaped isle, (approximately 12kms from north to south and 10 from east to west), Donald discovered that Rhum was very far from the 'magical' land 'flowing with milk and honey' that his old shepherd friend had described to him in his childhood.

'My first impressions were that it was rocky, sour-looking land, and over-run by hundreds of deer and a score of semi-wild Highland ponies. Twenty years of neglect meant that

broken fences allowed them to roam free-range. Visiting his shepherd once a month he noted the sheep didn't look too happy. As by now it was winter, but not unduly severe, he thought this was due to 'acclimatisation'. When spring came though and the sheep began shedding their wool he realised that his 'calculated investment' was in a poor condition. The health of his flock worried him further when they didn't improve when the spring grass came through, moreover sheep had mysteriously disappeared without trace and the lamb crop was very low.

'By this time I had two shepherds and they and the estate's head stalker blamed the losses on the several pairs of golden eagles which nested on Rhum. Then, adding to my problems maggot fly struck the sheep, and I discovered that sheep ticks with all their attendant diseases still existed.'

**Donald Cameron, Glen Nevis, Fort William**

Any rose-tinted dreams Donald had nurtured of record breaking wedder lambs was replaced by a stark economic question. Would he really be wiser to give up?

'I thought over all the evidence and just wasn't convinced that the eagles were solely responsible for my loss in numbers, so I talked privately with a retired Rhum estate worker and he backed up all the old stories I'd been told about the thriving sheep stocks and heavy carcase weights. He also told me that deer numbers had doubled on Rhum since those good old days. Now I remembered seeing a great many dead deer that spring and realised that their numbers had grown far too high. This was the real problem and I knew the solution would make me very unpopular with

**Donald Cameron (1995) in Glen Nevis that he once farmed (now farmed by his son)**

the laird.'

Culling the excess deer was the only recourse and David approached the Agricultural Executive Committee winning their support to increase the numbers which could be shot annually. As anticipated this did not endear him to the wealthy owner who regarded Rhum as her personal playground. From afar she imperiously ordered that her boat was not to be used for off-loading any more of Donald's stock. His financial problems were compounded as he now had to hire his own boat to make the 18 mile trip from Mallaig.

'Despite all these setbacks I wasn't giving up. Instead I stuck my neck out and borrowed more money to increase my stock, and I hired a third shepherd. With three new families on Rhum the school role doubled and the island's social life blossomed. Everyone turned up to events in the farm steadings where we all danced to a wheezy accordion or an ancient gramophone.'

Donald had discovered the real 'magic' of Rhum. It was the raw beauty of the desolate isle and the warmth of the little community who lived and worked there. As the years wore on and war wreckage washed up on Rhum's shores Donald continued rearing his sheep and cattle free-range over the wild terrain, gradually seeing improvements…

'I never achieved the high carcase weights that I'd daydreamed about at that auspicious committee meeting, but by the end of the war I came out with a few thousand pounds more than I'd put in, and meat that wouldn't otherwise have been produced made its way into the butchers' shops for rationing.'

As Donald Cameron recalled, his venture on Rhum hadn't been such a rum deal after all!

**Footnote:** Sadly, Donald Cameron died earlier this year.

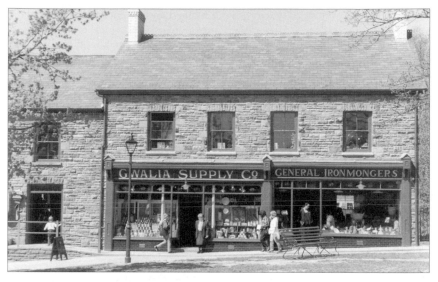

# How did they do that?
## *Moving Buildings*

WHEN you have been to one of the living museums around Britain which incorporates buildings which have been collected from other places, have you considered how the buildings were moved? We are not referring to copies or reproductions but actual buildings and materials which have changed location.

The first stage is to survey the building thoroughly, taking photographs, measurements and peering into the structure to see how it was made. Next has to be determined what parts of the structure can be saved and what repairs will be necessary. Also to be decided is the period of the property to be saved, as in most cases buildings will have been

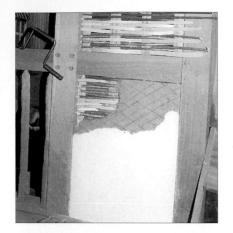

changed and extended over time. The next stage is to number and record every stone, or brick, and to fix numbered disks to every timber. The building can then be carefully pulled apart, and all the materials moved to the new site.

The construction is then carried out, from the information previously documented, using the actual stones, timbers or other materials in exactly the same position. With some designs some materials may have to be replaced, such as some wall designs, and thatched roofs but wherever possible, the same materials and techniques are used.

The photographs show some buildings that have been moved to the Welsh Folk Museum at St Fagans near Cardiff, and some examples of the techniques used in moving and reconstructing them. The work is continuous and extra buildings are still being moved.

# The Way We Used To Travel

## 1930 Road Traffic Act

ALONGSIDE the well-publicised disadvantages that might stem from railway privatisation, there could be the benefit of sensible train-bus connections of a kind that have not been generally enjoyed since 1930.

That was the year in which the Road Traffic Act was passed. Worried about the sheer power of the railways (though in truth their great days, commercially speaking, were already over), the government decided that railways should cease to be direct bus operators themselves but might invest jointly in bus companies. What emerged were decades in which the railways could neither effectively compete nor co-operate with road feeder services.

Until this point the railways had been expanding their bus mileage. Some feeder services had obviated the need to build expensive railways alongside roads in sparsely-populated country. Others ran first thing in the morning or last thing at night when there were no trains, or across-country linking stations on several routes.

As in so much else the Great Western was pioneer, starting a ser-

vice from Helston to the Lizard in Cornwall in 1903; that was a case where a costly railway had at first been planned, but could never have paid. Ultimately much of the GWR's territory was criss-crossed with its buses, after World War 1 painted in the same famous chocolate-and-cream livery as its train carriages. While there was a separate motor transport department, the local stationmaster was expected to take as much interest in the buses as the trains.

In the West Country, most GWR bus services were allocated to the new Western National (a separate East Devon-Torbay area was carved out to form the Devon General), while Southern Railway services became the Southern National.

Thereafter, if the railways wanted to replace a town service with a bus they had to charter it. The act did not stop the railways continuing to run their own air services, but now the chocolate-and-cream Great Western plane landing at what as optimistically called Torquay (in fact Haldon-above-Teignmouth) had to be met by a chartered Devon General bus.

But it was much worse than that. Outright train-bus competition was severely restricted, the joint owners

It is often forgotten that railways were major operators of bus services, the road-rail link connection now being made possible again by privatisation. The 1930 Road Traffic Act prohibited railways from running their own buses, of which there were sizeable fleets in the 1920s. The GWR had a policy of starting so many routes in certain areas that newcomers would be discouraged. But that was long after this bone-shaker which gave an exhilarating ride even at its permitted maximum 12mph had gone to the breaker's yard.

of the new bus companies objecting to something they did not like. That might mean the railways having to abandon a particularly cheap excursion, or the bus company changing its terminal from the railway station to town centre. Yet a request to retime a bus to make a better train connection might also be rejected.

This controlled competition in fact served nobody particularly well. It curbed creative enterprise all round, and encouraged both rail and road to act as though each had an inalienable monopoly. Certainly this

was a main reason why, in their later days, most rural train services were hopelessly out of keeping with the demands of the age. As a result they piled up such losses that ultimately only butchery of Dr Beeching could be seen as a 'solution'.

Politicians failed to take the point, but it was repeatedly said that what needed defending was an integrated transport system. It mattering relatively little to most people if the extremity of their journey were accomplished by rail or road providing there were through tickets with guaranteed connections and heavy luggage could be taken. Yet through tickets, connections and heavy luggage facilities were the last thing available. Indeed, it became customary for train and bus timetables to change on quite different dates.

Again, though never understood by the politicians of the day, the results were obvious to transport watchers. Above all, since neither the individual nor the co-ordinated benefits of train and bus were exploited, car ownership grew faster than necessary (and faster than in Europe) to the detriment of public transport as a whole. Yet simply because they did not keep pace with the times, failing even to introduce diesel cars on any scale until a decade after nationalisation, branch railways retained their old-time charm, and were run in the time-honoured manner until the only thing lacking was customers.

That the railways of the first pre-war period were so enjoyed and stimulate such nostalgia today is precisely because they were living museum pieces. There were steam engines pausing every thirty or forty miles to take water, signal boxes sometimes within sight of each other expensively controlling semaphore signalling, and at each station the stationmaster personally handing the pouch with the day's takings to the guard for conveyance to district office. The progress, often at an average of only

25–30mph, of stopping trains along lines of outstanding beauty, often on river banks, or across wild moors far away from roads, was as enjoyable as any entertainment.

The 1903 Road Traffic Act had various other ill effects. It created the concept of territorial bus companies, basically immune from the threat of competition, and acknowledged 'cross fertilisation', the use of excess profits on routes exploiting a monopoly to justify loss-making routes out in the sticks. Though the product of Conservative thought, it was the exact opposite of today's beliefs.

It also established the Traffic Commissioners, who pronounced on whether something was permissible or not. In the early postwar years this especially meant sitting in judgement on applications from long-distance coach operators to run services to the holiday resorts. Routinely such applications were opposed by the railways,

## The route of all evil

THROUGHOUT railway history there was bitter rivalry between the different routes, sometimes even when nominally they were run by the same people. Booking clerks not merely respected their customers' preferences but sometimes made their own assumptions... usually defending their own route against that of a rival.

At a West Country station they admitted to only one daily through train to Birmingham; it departed around lunch time which in winter meant an after dark arrival at Birmingham.

'Surely, there's a morning one; I'm sure I know somebody who used it,' pushed the would-be traveller.

'Only LMS. If you're prepared to go LMS, yes there is.' The clerk made it sound like Hell on wheels, and indeed Great Western boys cited 'LMS, Hell of a mess'. And if you were a country person, being disgorged in a noisy, sooty LMS New Street was altogether worse than arriving at the dignified GW Snow Hill.

who said their traffic would be unfairly affected at the start and end of the season while the coaches would not be able to relieve the peak load. Usually a compromise that might have seemed fair at the time (but in reality fudged the issue) was reached.

Sometimes disputes between bus companies were referred to the Traffic Commissioners, a famous example being the Gourd's case.

And then, of course, these were the days of the C-licence, enabling companies to buy lorries more or less without restriction purely for the conveyance of their own goods, but protection established road carriers such as Carter Patterson as well as the railways against the establishment of new carriers for any companies' goods. Again the effect was to pro-

**Grandma Gourd looks admiring on a bus of the type that ran the Bishopsteignton services for many years parked outside the firm's headquarters in Radway Street.**

long the established, traditional railway age and reduce the challenge to move with the times.

There is little doubt that the public were badly served. Even when the wholesale closure of branch railways began, virtually no effort was made to publicise connections or issue through tickets. The road operators generally ran replacement services so different in concept that even at their start only a third of the train passengers transferred, and many of them quickly deserted in the following months.

Sometimes things descended into sheer farce, with buses continuing to run down to a railway station years after the last train had left and, where trains still were running, the connecting bus arriving ten minutes too late for years on end. As a television reporter, the writer once showed how the bus from Kingsbridge (there was still public payment to provide a feeder service) arrived just after the

tail lamp of the last train for five hours had disappeared from sight. The worst thing was that both railway and bus operator wrote irritated letters rejecting the criticism as 'unconstructive', and the missed departure continued to be provided at public expense.

Such examples, and cases of railways being rebuilt when the last train ran, even of the last-ever train delivering a new fireplace to a station, were not uncommon. It remains to be seen what will be made of railway privatisation; that its seeds were sown in the malaise following the 1930 Act is for certain.

## A family affair

AS previously mentioned, the 1930 Road Traffic Act established territorial bus companies. The territorial company for East Devon through Exeter to Torbay was the Devon General, owned by British Electric Traction. The Traffic Commissioners had to decide which established small operators might survive, and summarily dismissed a defence by a Sidmouth operator simply because he spoke out in public... and thus lost his livelihood.

The case presented by a small company called Gourds, based in Bishopsteignton, Devon, was livelier. Founded in 1899, when a horse and cart were acquired to carry laundry boxes with passengers riding alongside the boxes for fourpence between Bishopsteignton and Teignmouth, the firm had grown as a family affair. The Traffic Commissioner chose to

attack the woman proprietor. 'Isn't it true that some of your buses carry only two or three passengers and wouldn't be missed?' shouted the commissioner, banging the rail. Mrs Gourd banged back that sometimes the Devon General ran empty.

Gourds survived, though were limited to their existing network of Teignmouth-Bishopsteignton-Newton Abbot and debarred from the main road bypassing Bishopsteignton. People walked from the main road to the village to save the penny difference between Gourds and the Devon General.

Many years passed, the Devon General and Gourds seemingly having their ordained roles to play, when a bolt from the blue arrived from the Devon General in 1949 (see page 70). Research by the BET's head office, had shown that the Devon General started operating over the last mile into Newton Abbot, from Kingsteignton, ahead of Gourds, who would have to withdraw. That was thirty years after their service had started.

The Devon General appealed to the Traffic Commissioners, who 'defended' the territorial company by attacking Gourds along the lines that 'they would surely like to make more profit... yes or no?' When they grudgingly admitted yes, they were 'helped' by being forced to charge twice as much on the Kingsteignton-Newton Abbot sector, 2d instead of 1d. Everyone realised it was a vicious decision, as were so many under the Road Traffic Act. In fact Gourds benefited: their buses carried large banners of protest, and the independent-minded people of Devon started to deliberately miss Devon General buses so they could pay twice the fare on the local one.

This naturally irritated the Devon General, and the outcome was that the Gourds were invited to lunch at the Torquay hotel (also owned by BET) and offered a 'ridiculous' price for the licence to be transferred. The last Gourd's bus ran on 1 January 1951. That evening the family lacked the customary enthusiasm to count the day's takings.

## Who needs passengers?

IT was advertised as 'passenger' but in truth carried far more goods than people. The last down-train of the day, with tight London connection at the junction, was never a great timekeeper. When it was seriously late the overtime paid to the signalmen at each 'crossing' station down the branch line must have exceeded the fares of the handful of passengers that were its normal human cargo. Only on Friday evenings, with young people who had taken London jobs returning to spend weekends at home, and especially just before Christmas and Easter, would you normally find more than a solitary person per compartment.

The guard's van was another matter. Items for each of the dozen or so stations needed careful stowing to ensure they were conveniently placed. At busy times, parcels overflowed into a couple of the adjoining compartments.

Baskets of pigeons, bottled gas cylinders, Harris sausages and Lyons cakes, calves and day old chicks, rabbit empties, trees and

## Charity began... at the ticket office

ASK some people what their favourite charity used to be, and if they answered honestly it would be their local railway station. Hoping their patronage might prevent closure, and perhaps leave the village with a through daily train to London, many used the station when the journey would have been cheaper or quicker by bus or car. Sometimes working closely with the village porter, whose job would certainly be lost if the station closed, such rail fanatics even canvassed friends to boost local traffic.

Especially was this the case during the week of the annual census. A different week most years, this was the time when every human arrival and departure, and by which particular train, was carefully noted and sent to headquarters. The really keen greatly increased the number of journeys they and friends made, even breaks of journey being carefully recorded. Headquarters must have marvelled at the difference between stations' revenue and the level of passenger patronage. Just what difference the census returns made was never known, but what more could you do to keep your village on the map than be counted coming and going?

shrubs in the planting season, private parcels of every conceivable shape and size, and of course mail bags kept the guard busy all the way down.

At each station, it was the signalman's duty to collect the passenger tickets and wheel the parcels to the parcels office as well as do his signalling. At a typical station, on most evenings only a postman was beside the signalman to greet the train. But farmers sometimes waited for their calves or day old chicks, although sometimes the signalman had to stay behind until a farmer, unsure when his 'goods' would arrive, had responded to a telephone call and driven hastily to the station. Even after the war many farmers made their cross, being unable to sign their names on the 'parcels received' register.

Every night, several baskets of carrier pigeons had to be released, and the time noted. These were birds in training. Today it is thought cruel to make them 'home' at night, but nocturnal flights were then taken for granted.

The last parcel entered up, the signalman wound down the platform's oil lamps from their brackets and extinguished them, waited for 2 bells pause 1 bell, train out of section, from the next station, rang up the closing-down signal, extinguished the oil lamp that lit up the lever frame, locked the door and put the key under the mat for his mate on early duty, only five or six hours away. Then home.

The pay was poor, the hours long, but it was not a bad life, for the previous train was two hours before, and the one before that two hours earlier again, leaving plenty of time for reading and a visit to the nearby pub, or earning a bob or two repairing bicycles and (in summer) tending the lineside allotment or going rabbiting with the dog. Mainline signalmen, only slightly better paid, had much more of a raw deal.

There was also great companionship in the branch line's social life. Signalmen listened in to conversations between others on the 'omnibus' circuit serving all boxes, though there was a separate, private circuit between adjoining boxes. Newspapers and magazines would be sent with the single line token to the next box and might be read by half a dozen different men during the course of a day. Plants and gardening materials were exchanged... and of course that essential staple cider sent to boxes not favoured with a local pub, the empty and payment coming back on the next train. A milkcan full of tap water was even sent to the next station down whose supply was erratic in the days before the mains. With all this activity, who missed passengers? – *David St John Thomas*

---

**The Way We Used To Travel**

**Do you have interesting recollections of old country transport? If so, send your 'Reflections', together with photographs to: Country Origins, PO Box 4, Nairn IV12 4HU.**

# The Chemist, Pharmacist or Apothecary

## *A look at a trade*

THE role of producer of medicines goes back to before recorded history and in Greek legend, Asclepius, the god of the healing art, delegated to Hygieia the duty of compounding his remedies. She was his apothecary or pharmacist. The physician-priests of Egypt were divided into two classes: those who visited the sick and those who remained in the temple and prepared remedies for the patients. In ancient Greece and Rome and during the Middle Ages in Europe, the art of healing recognised a separation between the duties of the physician and those of the herbalist, who supplied the physician with the raw materials from which to make the medicines. The Arabian influence in much of Europe during the 8th century AD, however, brought about the practice of separate duties for the pharmacist and physician. The trend toward specialisation was later

reinforced by a law enacted by the city council of Bruges in 1683, forbidding physicians to prepare medications for their patients.

In Britain, apothecaries are recorded back over the centuries, and mentioned in the time of King Edward the Third. The name means in Latin the keeper of a store. The earlier apothecaries prepared not only herbs and medicines but were also involved in the preparation and storage of preserves for the table particularly fruit in sugar, and were often also grocers. Many a large house had its own apothecary, who had very little routinely to do with medication, and was more involved in producing sweet items and preservatives, so perhaps they should have been called confectioners.

It was around the time of King James the First, that the apothecary appears to have given up the other arts to specialise in medicine. Up to this point physicians had generally prepared their own medicines, but from here on physicians generally did the diagnosing and prescribing and the pharmacists did more of the manufacture and dispensing. At this point there does not appear to have been any motivation for this in Britain other than convenience.

The Society of Apothecaries was formed in 1617, and had at around the end of the 1700s and probably for some time before, a hall near to Bridge Street, Blackfriars, London that housed two magnificent laboratories, out of which surgeons' chests for the British Navy were supplied. They also sold preparations direct to the public. Members were obliged to make their medicines and preparations, according to the formulas prescribed in the college dispensary. This was an attempt to raise standards. They also employed censors to visit members' shops, and destroy medicines that they did not think were up to standard. The records of the Society of Apothecaries are now in the Guildhall library in London.

In 1712 the profession was acknowledged in an act of Parliament which exempted for a period apothecaries serving as constables, scavengers, and other ward and parish officers, and from sitting on juries. A later act made these privileges permanent.

In many places the first apothecaries' shops were established at public expense. Some firms set up apothecaries in gardens, which grew all or most of the plants needed.

At the beginning of the 1800s, young people who wanted to be apothecaries had to be able to read

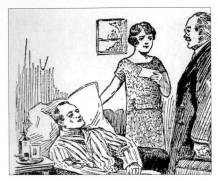

Latin, and have a grasp of the sciences. The apprenticeship lasted eight years. An assistant or journeyman who worked for an apothecary would have been paid around £40 a year out of which a deduction would normally be made for his board. At this time apothecaries were still in many places visiting the sick and giving them medicines as well as dispensing for physicians.

The work involved a fair amount of skill, not only in getting the ingredients right but in their preparation. Pills, for example, were made by grinding up the ingredients to a very fine powder and after mixing thoroughly, compressing them into each of the small holes on a mould, and making them sufficiently firm so that they could then be extracted from the mould without disintegrating.

The Pharmaceutical Society was formed in 1841, and its archives are in its offices at 1 Lambeth High Street, London SE1 7RN.

Moving forward in time a little, the chemist's shop of around 1900 often had other sections. It was not unusual for there to have been a dentist's in one part and an optician's in another. They had very large distinc-tively-shaped glass jars, known as carboys, round at the bottom with tall thin necks. Symbols of the chemist's profession, they were, like the signs on banks, pubs and pawnbrokers, necessary before the majority of the population were literate. Today they are also used to show the depth of history of the profession. The carboys are filled with coloured water, to symbolise the elements considered of importance in early times: green representing the earth, yellow for air, red for fire and blue for water.

Many of the museums with reconstructed shops display a chemist or apothecary's shop, and a particularly good example can be found at the Blists Hill open air museum at Ironbridge. This is a representation of a community around 1900, and the chemist's shop is a replica of one at Wellington, Telford, with all the shop fittings from a shop in Bournemouth. It has both a dental and optician's section.

Even well into this century many people would have gone to their chemist for advice and medication. Before the introduction of the National Health Service in 1948, there was a cost involved with calling on a physician, if you were not covered by the state insurance scheme.

The development of the pharmaceutical industry since World War 2 led to the discovery and use of new and effective drugs. It also changed the role of the pharmacist. The scope for on-site preparations of medicines greatly reduced and with it the need for the pharmacist's skills in the preparation of bougies, cachets, pills, plasters and potions.

# Geoff Hamilton's Country Origins

*John Kenyon*

IN THE early 1950s on an RAF Establishment 'somewhere in Germany' two young men shared the responsibility of running the station pig farm. The pigs did well, on the swill from the kitchens and the contents of the tins past their 'eat by' date. Occasionally there were sardines by the hundredweight, extricated from their packaging with a bill hook.

The RAF had chosen their 'managers' with care – these boys had the background for the job. What the RAF found difficult was making sure that any punishment for a misdemeanour was visited on the right one. The problem was that they were identical twins. Geoff and Tony Hamilton.

They were born in the East End of London, but at two had moved to what was then the country village of Broxbourne near the top end of the Lea Valley. (Now it is at the top end of the built up London sprawl.)

Geoff is told that he was interested in the garden at the age of four, but has no memory of it. Of course, it was a time of Dig for Victory – victory and a good cheap family diet. At six he does remember he and Tony getting a small patch each, and they grew their veg with the enthusiasm that close competition sparks in everyone.

They did everything together and before they were eight they knew exactly what they wanted to do – Tony would be a farmer, and Geoff would be a gardener.

Their friends, fellow pupils at Browbourne School, were sons and daughters of the growers and farmers of the Lea Valley. The twins spent all available hours outside, roaming everywhere, doing things that our children and grandchildren no longer can do: gang battles with cauliflower stumps as ammunition, and best of all, weekends living off the land in the fields and woods, armed with axe, knife, spade and blankets. They built shelters, roofed with ferns, fronds and

...two of a kind... early days

Henry Brewis

sods. Never waterproof, not always on high ground, some nights were miserable. They cheated on SAS style rules a bit; rabbits and pigeons were cheap and vegetables came from the garden, but they caught perch and eels, and cooked the lot on their forest fire. A proud boast is that they took only one pot, for tea, and everything else had to be manipulated over the fire on a twig, knife, spade. Real macho country oiks they were. There was not much else to do, but as Geoff says again and again, they loved it.

Aged ten Geoff got published in the *Children's Newspaper*! The article was not on parsnips and shallots, his preoccupations then were with pirates and ships. But it was the preface to journalism and to all those books.

There is another indicator to his future. His father was a buyer of junk lots, and amongst one of them was a pair of size eleven despatch rider's boots.

He had a tender obsession, his skinny legs. The young lad clumped around in them for years, they were his 'gear'. Macho, and masking his perception of a problem. Recently, in a pageant to celebrate the National Trust Centenary, he protected his public image yet again. His period costume included, at his vehement insistence, not hose but thigh length leather boots.

He went to Hereford Grammar School, were a Polish biology master introduced him to plant trials. Grow some seeds, divide them into groups. Give more fertiliser to group A, different light to group Z. Young G.H. became really hooked. His mother,

teachers and peers said he had to aim for University, which at that time meant Wye College. He viewed a prospectus, and decided that if he managed to get there he would be trained as a scientist. He did not want to be a boffin, he wanted to be a gardener. His father agreed that if he was set on an outdoor life, then he had better train for one. So when he left school he worked for a year on a nursery, followed by those two years National Service in the RAF, then Writtle College.

That friendly fellow who appears on Friday nights on BBC2 tv to tell you what to do in your garden has country origins, very influential ones.

He was taught to turn over the garden soil before Christmas every year, and to spread farmyard manure all over it, because in Broxbourne, in those days, there was lots of it about. He spent part of each day on that farm in Germany moving it, and the Barnsdale garden that blooms so wonderfully for all of us to enjoy is plastered with it.

There was one profound change from the past. The boy who once made collections of birds' eggs and butterflies, and later sprayed his garden with weedkillers and insecticides, became a powerful advocate for conservation and organic gardening.

Geoff has presented *Gardeners' World* since 1980. One wonders – has the BBC, like the RAF, ever been confused? Has Tony ever fronted the programme?

**We learned of the sad death of Geoff Hamilton as this issue was going to Press.**

## REFLECTIONS

# Avening's Pig's Face Day

*HOW many villages can boast a Pig's Face Day? Avening in Gloucestershire has two – or at least, two traditions, two rituals, totally different from one another, but both happened on 'Pig's Face Day'. The origins of the first are unknown, but certainly, from the beginning of the century, all the pubs in the village – the Cross and the Bell, the Nag's Head (in the hamlet of the same name), the New Inn and the Rising Sun – provided free sandwiches on Pig's Face Day, the Sunday following 14 September. Vi Townsend described how popular it was:* 'People used to come from Nailsworth, Horsley, all around – it was absolutely packed!…' *For the children, it was great excitement to see so many people in the village. Rose Simmonds, daughter of Ellen Ockwell, who lived in the little hamlet of Nag's Head, can take up the story. When did she remember it?*

'… Right back when I was a little girl! My Mother used to have a big electric boiler as she had in the back wash-house, and she used to cook about five pigs' heads, do it all out and put in a big container as brawn. Someone would collect it from her – she'd done it as a kindness – they'd collect it from her, how they issued it out I don't know, but every pub used

to do these brawn sandwiches, and that was all free. All the sandwiches was free – but people used to come just for a pig's face sandwich – oh, coachloads! They used to come in droves! No-one could never park! But I'm going back quite a long time, to my childhood, mind. It was really marvellous, it was a great day out, like Gatcombe!…'

*Don Teakle, formerly Chairman of the parish Council, recalled how much*

**Carrying in the Pig's Head at an Avening Feast. (Unfortunately we do not know who the photographer was.)**

*everyone enjoyed it:'*... We always had Avening Silver Band used to go round the village and play, used to play at Nag's Head, then come back and play at the Cross, and then they used to go down to the Bell, where those people did the same thing – made loads of sandwiches – people went without their meal in the day, so as to gave a good feed at night, you see...'

*Jim Halliday, who farms nearby at Hyde, also used to enjoy the evening celebration: '*... There was a pig up on the side with an apple in its mouth – I remember seeing that in there – at the Cross at Avening, in the evening, Sunday evening... It was all right! There was some singing going on there, oh yes!... You'd get there about 8 o'clock time on the Sunday... I was trying to think how long ago it was, but I can't remember!...'

*But what was it all about? Avening is an ancient settlement – there were ancient barrows at Nag's Head, so powerful or so significant to local people that in the early 19th century, they were moved away from a field called the Norns to be nearer the Church and the rectory in the village itself. Avening is built on the sides of two hills – oddly called Sunground and Moonground – the names but not the significance remain. In the early middle ages, it had a great wood (and, no doubt, wild boars) and a hawkery. It was part of the extensive lands of the Saxon lord, Brictric, and was transferred by William the Conqueror to the Abbess of Caen. And Pig's Face Day? The first we hear of it is in a little booklet written by A.S. Morris, published in 1911 by the Stroud News office and called 'The*

*Story of Avening'. It starts with the familiar story that Queen Matilda, before she married King William, met Brictric in Flanders and fell in love with him, but that he did not return her love. At this point, as Jill Adams of the Avening Parish History Group explained to me, Morris's story puts Avening centre-stage, saying that Brictric lived at Avening Court, and that it was the Queen, (having married King William by this time), who was responsible for Brictric's loss of favour – and lands:*

'... She still harboured some resentment against Brictric, and she asked King William to have Brictric arrested and thrown into jail, where he languished and died. Of course she was immediately struck with remorse and asked for a Church to be built in Avening in his memory, so to speak, and it is thought that when the Church was complete, a Feast was held...' *Was this the origin of the Pig's Face sandwiches and all the jollity at the Cross and the Bell? By the 1940s, the Church had appropriated whatever significance it had. Georgie Edmunds described what happened:*

'... In about 1949, the Rev. Cuthbert Cooper came to the village... and he looked up all the history of the Church, and he found that there was a feast given to the builders of the Church by Queen Matilda, and so he revived it, and we re-enacted it every year for many years... and the Hall was decorated – no electric light, all candles. We tried to do it exactly as it would have been done in 1080...'

*Elizabeth Buchanan and her husband came to the village in 1976, and remembered the same care and atten-*

tion to detail in the Feast in the 1980s:

'... People contributed their pewter tankards to decorate the table, which was beautifully laid out with cobb nuts and fruits of the season, and there was a candle-lit supper. Young girls from the village dressed up and served...'

*Jill Adams had been one of the serving-women, but remembered it somewhat less distinctly, because spectacles were considered an anachronism, so she and other short-sighted people had had to do without their glasses: people who usually wore glasses, were unrecognizable, and of course, could not see very clearly, themselves! The main characters in the drama were always present, dressed in proper early medieval attire, at the top table, and everyone who ought to have been there was there: the Rector of Avening, some Norman nobles, a Cardinal, the Archbishop of Canterbury, Queen Matilda, herself, her ladies-in-waiting, and her daugh-* ter, the Abbess of Caen. Different people would take on these roles each year. Georgie Edmunds, who as secretary of the PCC, organised the Feast many times, takes up the story:*

'... It would usually be in the dark by the time the Church Service was over, and we'd get all the people in the Hall, and ... a fanfare would be sounded... and they came in carrying these flaming torches. This was the first procession, when the Queen went up on the platform and made her speech. After they'd eaten, then the pig's head would be brought in to be presented to her, and they'd have another procession with these torches – and that's when Ron Coates would bring in this pig's head, because he was tall. He could hold it well up...'
*Jill Adams continues:*

**Making the sandwiches for Avening's Pig Face Day at the Bell In. (Photographer unknown.) Sydney and Nellie Tanner and their daughter Maureen.**

'... The boar's head was brought in on a platter, accompanied by two gentlemen carrying flaming torches. And they rushed in through the Hall with the flaming torches and the boar's head, and then exited by the side door – and apparently doused their flaming torches in the stream!...'

*In fact, of course, it was a pig's head, as boars no longer roam the woods about Avening. Not so long ago, everybody seemed to keep pigs in the village – William Cobbett, riding through in the early 19th century, said how important the pigs and gardens were in making people well-fed and healthy in spite of the slump in the woollen industry; before World War 2, there were pigs on the allotments in the hamlet of Nag's Head – but nowadays, there are more cars than pig-styes. Georgie used to get the pig's head from Nailsworth:*

'... There was a big factory at Nailsworth called Hilliers Bacon Factory, and I knew the Managing Director there. I asked him one day, could he possibly give us a *nice-looking* pig's head, and he did, every year afterwards. We always put an apple in its mouth and put some little bits of candles in for the eyes. Then we auctioned it, and people bought it, to take home to make brawn...'

*People remember with affection and admiration a play which Joyce Thomas wrote of the Avening story, called 'The Hawk Stoops', which was performed in the Church in 1980 for the 900th anniversary of the dedication of the Church – a play which evoked not only the medieval world, but also the beautiful landscape, the woods and valleys of the locality. But the older people remember perhaps most fondly, the earlier form of Pig's Face Day, when Avening was thronged with visitors. Don Teakle told me about Pig's Face Day in the hamlet where he lived:*

'... It was Mr and Mrs Jackson then in those days at the Nag's Head. They always did sandwiches, and people used to come from all the way round, Minchinhampton, Avening, Cherington – walking, they always walked. And they used to always sit on the stone walls on the left and on the right, and have their sandwiches and their pint of beer. They all enjoyed theirselves. We all went down and had a pint, or half a pint, and we also used to come along the Cross... The top room of the Cross was always – well, you had a job to move, in there. It was a good family get-together. Very often relations met that hadn't met for a long time... People used to come from Minchinampton, a lot of people used to come from Stroud, Nailsworth and all round there – lovely!...'

*Vi Townsend, Rose Simmonds, Don Teakle, Jim Halliday, Jill Adams, Georgie Edmunds and Elizabeth Buchanan told their memories of Avening Pig's Face Day to Jacqueline Sarsby of the Countryside and Community Research Unit, CGCHE.*

## Traditions

Does your area have special traditions or festivals? Why not write to Country Origins and tell us about them? Please send relevant photographs or artwork.

# Factory Farming, Medieval Style

*Graham Jennings*

THE variety and abundance of food available to us today from all parts of the world and the means of preserving it for consumption long after its production were pleasures unknown to medieval society.

Self-sufficiency was the order of the day and food was invariably home-grown or gathered from the wild.

The killing of small birds like thrushes and larks for the table was then as common here as it still is in some parts of continental Europe. They were limed and netted in great numbers both by the peasants and the sporting gentry.

The privileged landowners had both the legal right and the means to improve their own domestic economy by early forms of factory farming. Many manors and monasteries had fishponds, or 'stews', providing a variety of fish for the table, including eels and crayfish. The enclosure of deer herds into parks made venison available as required instead of relying on the fortunes of the hunt. Rabbits were often cultivated for food and fur in large, purpose-built warrens, or 'conygers'.

However, from the evidence of early statistics and the widespread survival of free-standing dovecotes in a variety of sizes and styles, the keeping of pigeons for the table seems to have been the most popular and widespread form of alternative meat production.

**Dunster, Somerset. Typical medieval circular tower dovecote, believed to be the oldest surviving example in Britain. Part of the monastic estate of the Benedictine Priory of Dunster. Retains interior revolving ladder, or 'potence'.**

Bruton, Somerset. Two-storied dovecote of the 12th-century priory. Taken over by the National Trust in 1922.

The Jacobean traveller, Fynes Maryson, noted in his account of Britain that 'no Kingdome of the Worlde hath so many Dove-houses'. Many of these charming utilitarian structures survive today throughout Britain. Often overlooked in reviews of our architectural heritage, dovecotes, also known as pigeon-houses, culveries or columbaria, display an intriguing variety of domestic architectural styles. Their durable quality of construction and the prominent positions they occupied among the other estate buildings, suggests that they were regarded as important and prestigious food production units in medieval high society.

Pigeons provided fresh meat in winter, in return for relatively little labour. The old birds at the turn of the year and the young squabs in spring relieved a diet of dried or salted meat. Their eggs were a tasty addition to the menu and pigeon manure was a free, and especially powerful, by-product.

The right to maintain a dovecote was a privilege reserved for the higher ranks of medieval society: manorial lords, monastic houses and parochial clergy. The extent to which this right was exercised is shown by the estimated total of 26,000 dovecotes in England alone in the 17th century. In Britain as a whole, the figure was probably nearer 30,000 and with an average capacity of 700 nesting-boxes per dovecote, there must have been over twenty million pigeons kept in purpose-built

**Bruton Somerset. Interior, showing nesting holes.**

accommodation alone.

Samuel Hartlib, a friend of John Milton, estimated that each pair of birds consumed four bushels of grain a year and he condemned the enormous waste involved.

To the tenant farmer, of course, whose crops provided free feeding-grounds for the landlord's birds, the pigeons were a destructive pest, but to kill them incurred severe penalties. No doubt he enjoyed great satisfaction in poaching for the family pot a pigeon or two grown plump on his own corn.

One of the demands made by disgruntled landowners who took part in the Pilgrimage of Grace in the reign of Henry V111 was that 'no man under the degree of knight of squire keep a dove-house except it hath been an ancient custom'.

The dovecote owners, always anxious to maintain or increase their stock of pigeons, devised schemes to protect them or to lure their neighbour's birds.

Whitewashing the exterior of the dovecote seems to have been an effective means of attracting other pigeons because it was an illegal practice at one time.

To keep birds from straying from their own dovecote, owners place inside a strange concoction called 'salt-cat'; it consisted of clay, salt, meal seed and a chopped-up cat, mixed together and baked. In the 13th century dovecote at Dunster in Somerset there are two trays around the central pillar which are thought to be the containers for this bait.

From the late 17th century, agricultural innovators such as 'Turnip'

Townshend and Coke of Holkham changed farming practice, enabling root crops to be cultivated and hay yields to be increased. It became easier to keep animals alive over the winter and fresh meat became available throughout the year.

The need for pigeon meat declined and no doubt this change and the continuing frustration of tenant farmers in having their fields stripped by their landlords' pigeons resulted in the Act of 1761/62, which allowed any landowner or freeholder to build a dovecote on his own land and any tenant to build one with his landlord's permission.

Significantly, few new conventional dovecotes were built after this date and most surviving examples are located in the earlier manorial or ecclesiastical sites. Some decorative dovecotes were built, especially on model farms, and other smaller pigeon lofts were incorporated into farm buildings.

As late as 1830, the naturalist Charles Waterton kept over one thousand pigeons in a round dovecote at Walton Hall in Yorkshire and used the droppings to manure his barley crop.

Dovecote design falls into three groups: the beehive, the lectern and the tower.

The beehive dovecote consisted of a cylindrical stone tower, narrowing at the top to an access hole, sometimes covered by a decorative cupola. These generally date from the 26th

*Opposite*: **Kings Pyon, near Hereford. Plaster and timbered dovecote in farmyard.**

*Above*: Naunton, Gloucestershire. A square, four gabled, stone-built dovecote with a roof of stone slates.

*Opposite*: The Butthouse, 1 mile south of Kings Pyon. Ornamented gatehouse (1632) incorporating a dovecote, in the courtyard of timber framed house.

century or earlier and there are a number of examples in the Scottish Lowlands.

The lectern type was built to a square, or double square, plan with a single pitched roof. Access was either by an unglazed clerestory in the roof

**Eardisland, five miles west of Leon-
minster. Brick-built, four gabled dovecote in grounds of 17th century manor
house.**

or by apertures beneath the eaves.
Lectern dovecotes are common in
Scotland but rare even in northern
Ireland and they date from the late
16th and 17th centuries.

The most common dovecote
design was the tower, varying in plan
from circular to octagonal and in roof
structure from conical to gabled on
two or four sides. Access for pigeons
was by dormer in the roof or by a
glover (a covered opening) at the
apex. In other examples there are
apertures near the top of the walls.

Materials and construction methods generally reflect the contempo-
rary architectural style of the area and
period in which the dovecote was
built. There are many good examples
of half-timbered dovecotes in the
Hereford and Worcester area, built
between 1500 and 1700. In other
regions brick, stone, flint, cobble and
even clay were used, with roofs of
thatch, slate and plain or stone tiles.

The interior walls of the dovecote
were lined with rows of nesting
boxes, usually with eight inch square
openings and a depth of fifteen inches.

Access to the boxes for the collection of eggs or birds ready for the
table was either by a portable ladder,
which was laborious, or more effi-
ciently by the installation of a
potence. This consisted of a revolving central axle extending to the full
height of the dovecote, with a pro-
jecting arm fixed at right angles near
the top. This either provided a move-

able support for the portable ladder
or had single or double ladders
attached to it.

Circular or octagonal dovecotes
allowed the easiest access to all parts
of the interior using this system, but
there must have been difficulties with
square buildings and in rectangular
dovecotes two potences would be
necessary.

Dovecote doorways were generally
low to prevent the birds from escap-
ing when access was required. The
step was generally raised above the
interior floor level to allow for the
accumulation of droppings.

As with many other vernacular
buildings which were erected to serve
the particular practical needs of a former rural society, dovecotes survive
in surprisingly large numbers but in
diverse states of preservation.

Many are neglected and crum-
bling; others, particularly on farms,
are used for storage or the shelter of
cattle; some, in private ownership
have been carefully restored as attractive architectural features in their
own right, often with a few decorative
fantails in evidence to remind us of
their formal use; a number are in the
permanent care of the National Trust
and open to view.

### Early Transport

Do you have interesting photographs of early motoring or public transport? If so, please send
them to us, with as much detail as
possible and we will try to include
them in a future issue of *Country
Origins*. Please mark all photographs clearly on the reverse
with your name and address

# Painting Farm Machinery...

BORN in 1946, into a family much involved with the Lowestoft fishing industry, artist Joe Crowfoot, naturally grew up with a great affection for the old steam drifters and trawlers, sadly now long since

*Farmyard*: **Ransomes threshing drum and elevator driven (by belt) from a Field Marshall single cylinder tractor. Tractor in background is a Fordson Major. painted at a farm in St. Michaels, nr Bungay, Suffolk.**

departed, that worked from the port during his childhood years.

His own early working life was spent on the barges used to maintain the Norfolk Broads. During that time he taught himself the mystic craft of making ships in bottles, followed by experiments with canvas and brush. In a very short time there was sufficient demand for his work, to consider it as a full time career.

As time went by, Norfolk wher-

**Field Marshall in tractor shed, Aldeby, Norfolk**

ries, steam trains, rural landscapes and aircraft paintings, extended his artistic appeal to a wider audience.

Joe's work has been exhibited throughout the eastern counties, as well as at London's Mall Gallery.

Joe has this to say about the inspiration for his paintings:

'My interest in farm machinery really goes back to my school days, living in a small village on the Norfolk-Suffolk border. In those days (the 1950s), it was much easier for children to get very close to the every day working on local farms and although I loved to see the heavy horses, my memory of them is always tinged with sadness because while I

was young, one of the horses that we all knew well suffered from a fit and had to be shot, by the side of the road, quite near to our school.

Tractors, on the other hand, could not suffer in any way and in the light of that incident, that was probably the reason I was drawn to all things mechanical.

The tractors of my childhood were wonderful creations with many of their working parts on view – always noisy and accompanied by the unforgettable smell of hot oil and T.U.O. They had wonderful names such as

*Overleaf*: *Harvestfield*: **David Brown 25 D tractor with international self binder. Painted at a farm in Ringsfield, Suffolk.**

Allis Chalmers, David Brown, Fordson Major and Field Marshall.

Of all their annual tasks, I found myself most drawn to ploughing and harvesting. Walking to school on many a cold, misty autumn morning, there would be an old 'High Major' struggling to plough a heavy clay field, followed by a white plume of relentless seagulls.

Then, as a complete contrast there would be a golden summery harvest field with that same tractor, this time with an old, self binder, that kept on breaking down because it was only designed to be pulled slowly behind horses – and the sheaves of corn stacked all round like tepees in the Wild West.

In my paintings, I try to show such scenes but also the more negative side. Tractor driving in those days was uncomfortable, tedious, dangerous and often very cold work. I have seen men unable to stand up after many hours ploughing, with sacks tied around them in an attempt to stave off the cold and wet.

Many of the machines featured in my paintings belong to friends and are still used to recapture something of the old times at ploughing, harvesting and threshing events throughout the year and I am glad to say that they are not kept in showroom condition but with all the rust and grime that they have so proudly carried all through their working lives.'

For further information about Joe Crowfoot's work, tel: Tudor Galleries, Norwich 01603 713350.

**Standard Fordson ploughing at Brompton, Suffolk**

## REFLECTIONS

# Life at the Bobbin Mill

*IT is almost seventy years since Tommy Richardson began his working life at the Low Briery Bobbin Mill, Keswick. Now at the age of 85, and still 'lish' [fit], Tommy is arguably the last survivor in the town, of an industry that once employed thousands of people throughout the Lake District.*

*In the middle of the 19th century, 120 water-powered mills in Cumberland and Westmorland produced almost half of the bobbins that were required for the world's textile industry.* 'Ivvery laal village had a bobbin mill in old days. Aye we sent bobbins all over t'world.' *remembered Tommy.*

*He pointed towards some grey, stone cottages.* 'I was only four year old when I went to live down yonder. I went to school from there, an' when you got to fourteen, and left school, you got a job in t'factory you see. We lived in t'firm's houses, so that was it. The lads just got any jobs to do, but I was lucky and was taken on as a bobbin turner, and I had to serve my time with that for a lot of years to learn the trade. They only needed so many apprentices so I suppose I was lucky. They used to employ about 120 so it was a big thing for Keswick. It kept Keswick ga'an.'

*Down at his former work place he looked over what has been transformed from an industrial site into a modern caravan park. Low Briery is in a sheltered hollow, and surrounded by trees,* much of which is the remainder of formerly coppiced woodland. 'There'd be a great pile of wood up there, you know, trees, and there'd be big cranes swinging timber on to laal [little] bogeys to run down rails to the saw shed. There was plenty of timber already here, but they used to import wood, that timber called teak, but it was mostly local wood d' y' know. In among teak we sometimes used to git greenheart, that's a foreign timber like. Now and again they'd git an odd piece that had been shoved in by mistake in among all this teak. I could sometimes git a bit o' that greenheart for mekin' a fishing rod. Most o' t' wood used to come in green, they bought it out o' t' woods. They had their own wood cutters chopping trees down. These fellas would go along, mebbe three o' them,

**Low Briery Bobbin Mill workforce about 100 years ago**

wid a wood wagon, and there would be three horses pulling this wood wagon, and they would laid it up and bring it back wid a load o' timber. That was in the early days, then after that they got what is known as a traction engine, to pull the wagons.

There was about six different piles of timber and six different cranes. Cranes was med o' wood in them days; great big beams o' wood about twelve inches thick. They would hold anything nearly. You'd twine a handle down here somewhere, and it lifted a tree up to take it on til a bogey to run it down on t'railway lines into the saw mill.'

*There, the saw machinery which was driven by the power generated by the fast flowing river Greta, would cut the rough timber to size before it went to the drying sheds.*

'We called them kilns where the wood went to dry out an' all that. Aye, it all had to be dried properly, properly dried as you might say before it could be used. Then when it was ready, it came into the turning sheds where it was cut into different size bobbins. There was all different machines set up to make the different sizes, it was something like a lathe. Different kinds o' bobbins was med from different wood, well you got different thicknesses, do y' see.'

*The Low Briery site was compact, and unobtrusive to the environment by its screening of trees. The 'turning sheds' were adjacent to the saw sheds and the kilns, to complete the complex. The nearby steam boiler house provided the heat for drying the wood.* 'They used to mek their own gas. We'd a gas engine. We used to git gas from the timber

waste, and this used to help out with a bit o' power, but in the old days, the whole mill used to be driven with water from t' river. To start it off, you'd to go up to the top o' the mill race, and turn so much water on to the weir, but later on, gas and electric took over altogither.'

*The finished wooden bobbins were then taken to the nearby goods yard of Keswick railway station from where they were transported initially along the rails of the Cockermouth, Keswick and Penrith Railway, to supply the cotton and woollen industries of Lancashire and Yorkshire.*

'There used to be a laal station at Low Briery once over. Aye the train used to stop here every morning for the workers to get off that had come from Cockermouth or Keswick, then it would be back again at half past five to take them home.'

*Tommy still has a collection of differently shaped wooden bobbins that show the great variety that were made.* 'I just kept them as souvenirs. This 'un was a reel for fishing line. Aye, we used to make these, then they used to fill them with what was used for fishing line, and sell them. T'others was there for wire, and wool and cotton and whatever was needed. We used to make some that was long enough for carpets to go on. Some of the bobbins was big enough to sit on, like stools you might say. I suppose I was sort o' lucky, I used to move about a bit on different jobs, but some on the fellas used to git on one machine and work that, and that was it. At end o' t'day you all got same wage so it didn't matter a damn whether you were any good or nut. You only got Union rate o' wages and that was it.'

Tommy worked for the mill when it was owned by Coward Phillipson Co. Keswick, and proudly recalled that although the wage for a time served bobbin turner was £3. 1s 6d for a 48 hour week, his mill was the first to work a five day week in the Keswick area. 'And there was no reduction in wages for the five day week. On the Friday night, you'd all line up, over there. You all had a number you know. They shouted your number out and you got your pay in a laal tin box.'

When the bobbin mill closed in June 1959, Tommy had worked there for 34 years, but the next 24 brought a change of scene, and a change of climate; 'I managed to get a job in slate quarry carry on, it was cold on top of Honister, hell it was cold; it was a big change for me, 'cos inside at bobbin factory, it was warm and dry.'

The Greta, that runs past Low Briery, has seen other industries on that site, for although its water is ever changing, the power of the river has been used for industrial purposes for over six centuries. Bobbin making was not the only industry practised here for a pencil mill and a textile mill for making intricate bottom edgings for waistcoats also occupied the site. The latter gave the area its local name. 'Aye, they used to call it Fancy Bottom down here, but it was t' bobbin mill that brought work to Keswick. Aye, when it was busy there would be 40,000,000 bobbins gaan out o' Fancy Bottom ivery year.' Even the bobbins for holding the threads used for making the Coronation gown of Queen Elizabeth II were manufactured at Low Briery. The last thirty years have wrought great changes to this former industrial site. Seeing the ranks of the neatly sized caravans in what is now a holiday village, it is hard to imagine the former scene of industrial activity. The once high pitched screams of saw blades have now been replaced by a chorus of bird song. Tidy stretches of a tarmacadam parking area cover what was once the floor of the turning shed, littered with curled shavings from the spinning blades that shaped the bobbins. The joiner's shop has gone, a new toilet and washing block has taken its place. 'It wasn't like that in my day, we had board with about four holes spread along it, opening on to the earth. A fella used to come along with a cart, and shovel muck over it.'

The station has disappeared; all that remains is the raised mound of a stone edged platform alongside a public footpath, which has become a popular and attractive walk. Three old photographs within a telephone kiosk, and an information board beside the footpath are all that remain to tell the tale. Faded faces show unsmiling expressions below flat cloth caps, as they look out from the formal photograph of the work force, where some of the faces were familiar to Tommy; 'This is the ambulance fella, he used to bandage you up when you cut your fingers; I knew quite a few of these. I was nobbut a lad then, and they had been there a while.'

Had he any regrets about the mill's closure, and the changed nature of the site?

'Oh dear no. Ivverything's got to mek progress, hasn't it. That's the way of the world.'

Tommy Richardson was talking to Sheila Richardson (no relation!)

# The Drovers' Road from Wales to England

*Victor Terry*

OVER a period of a thousand years Black Welsh Runts cattle, sheep, pigs and geese were gathered at collecting points in Wales. The large herds were then driven along the Drovers Roads across the Welsh mountain ranges to the livestock markets in England. Markets and cattle fairs were held along the drovers' route at various locations. Newent was granted an annual Cattle Fair and weekly market to the Norman Abbot of Cormeilles in 1253. The cattle trade is recorded on Spoad Hill on the Radnorshire-

**The Drovers Restaurant, Market Place, Llandovery. The collecting point for the droves providing accommodation and refreshments for the drovers before setting out on the long journey. O.S. 146/767343.**

The route of the drovers' road on top of Bryn Mawr looking towards Esgair Gelli in the Cambrian Mountains. O.S. 147/801574.

Herefordshire border where gaps were left in Offa's Dyke, the ancient earthworks constructed by the Mercian King Offa in 780 AD.

In 926 AD an agreement was drawn up between the English Witan tribe and the Dunsaetae tribe of Wales concerning the border arrangements across the lower reaches of the River Wye. It strongly indicated a legitimate cattle trade and established cattle tracks on both sides of the River and made reference to the consequences of a track being wrongly followed. The ordinance was drawn up by King Athelstan.

The drovers approaching Hereford would cross the old bridge into the City of Hereford where the cattle market is still held today. They would buy or sell cattle before going on towards Warwickshire. The photograph was taken from the new bridge that bypasses the city centre. O.S. 149/505402.

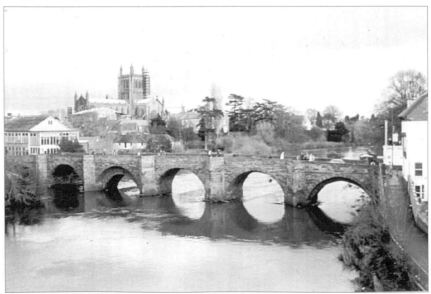

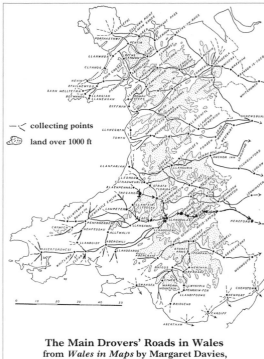

**The Main Drovers' Roads in Wales**
from *Wales in Maps* by Margaret Davies,
University of Wales Press, 1958.

could be seen by drovers approaching an area. In England three yew trees marked similar places of rest. Various ale houses and inns bore the name of the 'Drovers Arms' or 'The Drovers' along the routes and at the collecting points. The ruins of the 'Black Ox' public house lie somewhere on the Clyro Hills that were visited by drovers before reaching Rhydspence where there was a Welsh Inn on one side of the stream and an English Inn built in 1350 on the adjoining side with a smithy. The Welsh Inn is now a private house and the English one is known as the Rhydspence Inn with an old horse-operated cider press standing in the yard, which was used until 1956.

In Mid-Wales and South Wales, Tregaron, Pumsaint and Llandovery were typical collecting points before the Drove set off across the Cambrian Mountains, Mynydd Eppynt, fording the River Wye at Erwood, crossing the Clylo Hills to the Hereford plain and on to Warwickshire before going east to such markets as Northampton or South to Barnet Fair or Smithfield Market.

Along the routes, drovers' accommodation and refreshment houses were established with resting and feeding stations nearby for the cattle. In Wales a group of three Scots pines denote drovers' accommodation at farms and other establishments and

The well trodden drovers' roads/tracks were 14 ft wide and left a permanent pathway throughout the

Further Reading
*The Drovers Roads of Wales* by Fay Godwin & Shirley Toulson, Wildhouse, 1977.
*Wales and the Drovers* by Phillip Gwyn Hughes, The Golden Grove Book Company, 1988.
*The Welsh Cattle Droves* by Richard J. Colyer, University of Wales Press, 1976.
*Wales in Maps* by Margaret Davies, University of Wales Press, 1958.
*Understanding the Countryside – man's impact on landscape* by Ron Scholes, Moorland, 1985.

**The drovers' road at Cefri Cerrig, Cambrian Mountains. O.S. 146/762576.**

passage of time as beasts passed over them. They had large upright slabs of stone on the sides of the road or banks with hawthorn or blackthorn hedges. The drove from Tregaron via Hereford to Warwickshire in many places still bears the name of the Welsh Road or the Welsh Way, a journey which took some sixteen days to travel. The drove from Tregaron

**The old cider press that can be seen when visiting the Rhydspence Inn**

to Barnet Fair would have taken 23 days.

There is little evidence of the Half Penny Fields that were used for the grazing of cattle on the drove, or of the three scots pines/yews now existing. The Half Penny Field can be found on many local maps usually to the rear of inns, close to a farmhouse, or near a now derelict farm building. Visually they can be identified by the lush green nature of the well manured grassland – the result of the many thousands of cattle using the enclosure over long periods of time. The Talbot Arms at Tregaron had a Half Penny Field at its rear charging ½d a night per beast for its use.

The journey along the former drovers' roads today show modern communication systems, modern catering services like drinks vending machines, bridges replacing the river fords, and tarmacadam roads replacing the ancient drove tracks. Even so, much of the original routes still exist.

The signpost in Tregaron points to the mountain road most of which is the ancient drovers' road across the mountains. Shortly after leaving this village you see three scots pines at the entrance to a farm (now offering accommodation to caravanners). In Llandovery the market place has a Drovers' Restaurant and marked the collecting point of the droves.

At Pumsaint collecting point a shoeing station exists and at various points along the route. Due to the rough terrain, the cattle, sheep and pigs were all shod and even the geese had battens tied to their feet and then were run through a mixture of sand and tar to protect their feet. The cattle were fitted with eight cattle cues (one pair of ox tips fitted to each hoof). Some years ago many cattle cues were found in the silt at the old ford crossing of the River Avon at Chesford near Kenilworth in Warwickshire, at the point where the Welsh road crossed the river heading towards Southam.

The drovers' trade remained in existence for about a thousand years until the spread of the railway network into Wales in 1865. The railway companies at this time kept records of the number of cattle transported by rail (that obviously had been formerly driven on the drovers' roads) and recorded 695,796 cattle. The sheep, pigs and geese were also transported but were not counted by the head. Some cattle continued to use the drovers' roads for some years to come whereas other drovers found employment taking the cattle on the shorter routes to the rail heads and the rail collecting points. The towns and villages grew up around the railway and the cattle trade. This saw the demise of many towns and villages, hamlets and inns and accommodation establishments in isolated places and in the high mountains which had been reliant on the drove/cattle trade. Now, mere stone foundations with ruins of stone walled cattle enclosures remain as a relic of this era.

### *Museum*
*Welsh Folk Museum at St Fagans, Cardiff. Within a 100 acre parkland the lifestyles of the past, where Welsh people lived and worked, are reflected in a variety of authentic re-erected buildings from all parts of Wales. It has Black Welsh cattle, sheep and pigs. Tel. 01222 569441. (3 miles from Junction 33 on the M4 Motorway)*

## Useful Addresses

| | | |
|---|---|---|
| Youth Hostels Association Trevelyan House 8 St Stephens Hill St Albans Herts AL1 2DY | GB & Ireland 11 Grosvenor Place London SW1W 0EY | Ramblers Association 1/5 Wandsworth Road London SW8 2XX |
| Camping and Caravanning Club of | Ordnance Survey Romsey Road May Southampton SO9 4DH | Wales Tourist Board Brunel House Fitzalan Road Cardiff CF2 1UY |

## REFLECTIONS

# Yesterday's Country People

## Bill

BILL is possibly the only person ever to be featured in *Country Origins* who never once during his life stepped foot in the countryside Not, anyway, the British countryside. He did indeed experience months of mud in the trenches of World War 1, but even his journeys through Kent to the port were seemingly after dark.

Yet if there had been an electronic means of assessing who knew the most about the country, its ways, crops and their value, about land ownership, and just who was who out in the sticks, Bill would have been close to the top. His knowledge was, to say the least, surprising and increased daily as he practised it.

Bill was head waiter at one of those London hotels, patronised by out-of-town people, where Miss Marple would have felt at home. Though you did not have to prove you lived beyond the green belt to stay there, virtually all the regulars did. This was partly achieved by those living well away from the capital planning their journeys and making their reservations early and since, at peak times, the hotel was almost always full, there was no scope for others.

Though its floral decorations were perfectly acceptable, curiously the hotel had never set out to cultivate a particular clientele. Unless Bill himself was the unconscious perpetrator, it just happened. As for Bill, he would probably have excelled equally at any speciality as a kind of precursor of Trivial Pursuit.

He was not alone among his class in recognising most of his customers and their favourite seats, beverages and dishes, but took the art of flattery to what in hindsight must be regarded as an illogical extreme. In other words, he studied form. He combed *The Times* and even the farming press for relevant tips. He noted instantly who was being knighted or made an OBE. *Bradshaw's Railway Guide* was another essential reference tool; from it, he knew not only how long the train journey would take, but how many (if any) changes there would be and how long the road journey might be at the end. The exact location of each of his regulars was marked on a map from an old timetable, always scrupulously refolded. The red numbers referred to his private notebook in which he recorded the names, addresses and every other detail of his slice of Britain: the birth dates of children, size of landholding and, in the case of farmers, whether each season had been successful or not. Hunting, shooting and fishing he could converse about as though he had been brought up as a member of the landed gentry.

Of short stature, but with an increasingly bent back in his last thirty years, Bill must at some stage have concluded he had to do something to make his mark. he succeeded to the extent that when country people gathered for a hunt ball in Shrewsbury or over market day lunch at Durham, his name was frequently mentioned, not in awe or even perhaps especially in respect, but to indicate that the right choice of London hotel was made... the place where Bill presided over the dining room.

With his pulse on the rural economy, Bill could have forecast business trends better than any hotel manager, and could calculate to a nicety how much he would be likely to make in tips. Good seasons had him welcoming his guests as though their visits were a celebration; when times were lean, as often they were, he would exchange muted confidences about the impossible price of lamb and what New Zealand imports were doing, dropping a hint as to what someone from the same region (though never a close neighbour) had experienced. The art was always to flatter the guest by pointing out things were worse elsewhere. Such flattery yielded not only good tips but job security... and pheasants and grouse when top farmers and their wives came for the Smithfield show or the gentry for Christmas shopping.

Bill (now too old for service) stayed at his post throughout World War 2. There were strains, certainly, but enough regulars came even for short visits with 'thank you' rabbits and hares to satisfy his own needs and help the hotel's. Quite what the system was between Bill, chef and management nobody knew. – *David St John Thomas*

**Violet at the age of 21**

---

### Lady's Maid

BORN in 1902 in a mid Devon village, Violet had had a happy childhood going to the village school at the age of three and leaving at fourteen. 'I remember playing hockey with a plain stick – not the curved edge of today – and tennis on the courts of the old Rectory.'

On leaving school she took two entrance exams to St Lukes College and the Records Office in Exeter; passing both but hearing from the latter first, she spent many happy years there. Lodgings were found with one of the Sergeant Majors in the week and she became firm friends with his daughter, coming home at weekends. Recreation was in the

**First employment as a lady's maid in Somerset**

form of theatre in the week – sixpence in the gods to see Gracie Fields, Marie Lloyd, Nellie Melba and walking the seven miles to Crediton, with friends, at weekends often laden with shopping on the return journey.

When the war ended, she decided she needed a complete change and became a lady's maid to the Trevelyans at Willton, Somerset for two years. Then, in 1922, began a fourteen year employment and friendship with Lord and Lady Portsmouth who sought her out through interview and references from her employer and the Rector. The duties of a lady's maid were time consuming – realising her employer's needs before she had herself – putting out clothes needed for the day, before she had risen; washing and styling her hair and choosing jewellery to match each set of clothes. The day could be a long one starting at 8am and finishing at 1pm. If the lady had gone partying Violet would have to wait up in order to undress her ready for bed. They would also go shopping together in a car for clothes; sometimes to London, maybe Harrods, and at Christmas time Violet always dressed the tree and wrapped all the presents. She was her employer's companion when travelling to gentlemen's houses – Longleat was always visited three times a year as Lord Portsmouth and the Earl of Bath were cousins – although she never saw their 3,000 acre ranch at Wyoming as Lady Portsmouth had commented 'too isolated for you, Chanter'. Head servants were always called by their surname but Violet had always felt she was one of the family. She had come to the conclusion that the 'real old gentry' would always treat you with respect whereas the 'jumped up gentry' were best avoided. Any free time (which was not a lot) was spent writing letters, dictated by Lady Portsmouth, as her writing was so bad, and making all her silk underwear and blouses as well as tea gowns. The latter were worn when she wanted to dress down for the evening.

There were eight on the staff – two gardeners, odd job man, cook/housekeeper, butler/footman, two housemaids and laundry – and Violet had her own room called The Workroom but took meals in the Servant's Hall.

Towards the end of her long employment, Lady Portsmouth became ill with multiple sclerosis and despite seeing doctors and specialists became steadily worse, so Violet, with their blessing and money as a wedding present decided the time was right to leave and marry the farmer's son she had known for a long time.

They married in the village church, he dapper in a smart suit and she in a long, light blue dress with a lace edged hat – its brim turned up at the back and edged with rosebuds.

'My bouquet was a picture – a huge mass or carnations, orchids and lily of the valley with ferns trailing down like a waterfall. I had no bridesmaids as I preferred a quiet wedding. Our honeymoon was spend in Dorchester and then we started life on a rented 300 acre farm in Totnes. There were always two single men living in the farmhouse – one would have been learning – and one man in one of the two cottages on the land. The twenty-plus cows were milked by hand until a milking machine was purchased – the morning milk went to Paignton whilst the evening milk was made into 12lb cans of cream

(separated, scalded and then cooled by me) to go to a Farm Produce Shop at Torquay. We always had two collies who were never allowed in the house as well as the fourteen farm cats who were always fed with a bucket of bread and milk every evening as well as scraps from the table.

'My day would start at 5.30 – 6 o'clock with the men coming in for their fried breakfast of bacon, eggs, fried potatoes and toast at 8 o'clock.'

All her days were extremely busy as she also had her in-laws to cater for. In the summer, she was open for Bed and Breakfast and all her customers came by word of mouth – she never had to advertise – coming back year after year; some for only the night, others for two weeks. The longer stayers also had the pleasure of evening meals. Her farmhouse was huge – eight bedrooms – with high ceilings and a 23ft long mantlepiece in the kitchen/dining room; formerly

**Gathering in sheaves**

a library.

Before the advent of the Aga, a six gallon copper fountain filled with water was placed on the fire ready for use. Two rows of servants' bells, downstairs and up, added character to the house. Without a washing machine, washing took all day and was always done on a Monday – later a year's profit went into buying the labour saving device. Carpets were kept clean by using a dustpan and brush. Later still, to enhance the dining room a beautiful bookcase/bureau was bought costing £2.10s – the writing desk lined with birds eye maple.

'Our busy life did not allow for holidays – my husband wasn't keen on going away, so I took the odd day off.'

After thirty years of farming they left Totnes because of her husband's asthma and moved near Crediton. The village used to be so quiet, no traffic, only horse drawn four-wheeled carriages – although she can remember seeing the first car owned by the doctor – A Ford T.

There used to be eight shops including the bakers, Post Office and a few general stores as well as two pubs. Various businesses used to drop by once a week with their wares – some in open lorries – fishman, clothes/glassware, china from Barnstaple, household goods/ saucepans – everyone knew everyone else and their business and were probably related down the generations.

Now the village has outsiders from the cities and weekend homes, only one pub but the post Office is still

there, a butchers/Spar shop, a general stores, hairdressers and a doctors. – *Jane Partridge*

## Frewin, The Country Carrier

FREWIN GRAY was a country carrier for more than forty years. He was often to be seen travelling around the villages of East Leicestershire with his horse and covered van. He was a strong man with a ruddy complexion, acquired from many hours spent out of doors in all kinds of weather. He was born in 1891 in quite a large house at Houghton on the Hill in Leicestershire, next to St Catherine's Church.

His parents, Alfred and Annie Gray were very proud at the birth of their firstborn child, and when he was old enough to understand, Alfred Gray would take him to see the windmill which stood in a field by the side of the little lane which led to the Ingarsby Railway Station.

'I was the last miller to operate that mill,' he would say, and he would tell his son how many bags of grain would be ground into flour each day. It had been a sad day for his father in 1874 when he finished his work, and locked up the mill for the last time, because it needed far too many expensive repairs which the owner could not afford to be carried out.

Frewin loved the simple life of the village. When he was a small boy he knew the names of many of the wild flowers and trees which grew in the

**Houghton on the Hill windmill**

fields and woods nearby. He could recognise the songs of the birds, and towards the end of April would watch eagerly for the first swallows to arrive, and he would listen for the song of the cuckoo.

Before going to church on a Sunday, he would first take the joint of beef and the Yorkshire pudding to the nearby bakery to be cooked. Many of the villagers did this, fetching their meal later – all steaming hot.

Frewin attended the village school and was quick at his lessons, for he enjoyed learning. Sometimes he would be playing in the large garden of his house, and, on hearing the ringing of the school bell, would leap over the garden hedge and arrive just in time to take his place in the line of children in the playground, and file into the classroom.

Frewin loved horses and often when the doctor, who came from the next village some two or three miles away, rode into Houghton on horseback, it was Frewin who would run to take the bridle and hold the horse for the doctor.

Saturday was the highlight of the week for Frewin, for he was allowed to travel with his father on the van into Leicester. He was just ten years old when, one cold day in January 1901, he stood with his father and a crowd of people in Leicester's Municipal Square to hear Edward Prince of Wales proclaimed King Edward VII.

Frewin enjoyed the hustle and bustle of the town, and often his father would take him for a ride on a horse drawn tram.

Very occasionally a galloping horse pulling a fire-fighting appliance would come down the main road, and this would cause much excitement. There were always lots of horses and carts around, and in the centre of the town there were many blacksmiths. Often there would be a queue of horses waiting to be shod. Bread, milk and coal were delivered by horse and cart, and sometimes the horse would bolt, causing panic amongst the Saturday shoppers.

In 1904 electric trams first made their appearance in the town. These had no roofs on the upper deck, so passengers sitting there had no shelter in bad weather.

At the age of twelve, Frewin left school, having obtained his labour certificate the year before, and he was then able to help his father in the business.

In 1915 Frewin joined the army and served for two years in German East Africa, Egypt and Palestine. He spent some time in hospital in Cairo and Alexandria, but on 20 January 1919, Frewin arrived back at the little country station of Ingarsby, and set out to walk the mile or two to his home village glancing affectionately on the way at the windmill which was still standing, although in a decrepit state. Later that year Frewin watched with sadness as, bit by bit, the mill was pulled down. A historic landmark had gone for ever. A photograph of the mill which hung on the wall of Frewin's home became one of his most treasured possessions.

When Alfred Gray became too old to carry on with the business, Frewin took over. He knew well the routine of the life of a carrier. He would be up early in the morning, going round the villages nearby, taking orders from customers for merchandise they wanted from Leicester. Sometimes it was food they requested, or perhaps an article of clothing for a child. Frequently he would be given shoes to take to the cobblers to be mended. At times the local carpenter would require lengths of timber, or the builder would ask for bags of sand or gravel.

On days when there was a cattle market in the town, the local farmer would sometimes ask Frewin to bring back some hens or piglets, and on one occasion it was a young calf. Frewin collected large hampers of dirty sheets and other linen from some of the hotels, and these he would take to various registered washerwomen on his routes. He would return the linen to the hotels a day or two later all nicely washed and ironed.

The country carrier, travelling from village to village, picked up many pieces of local news. Frewin was very well liked by all who knew him, for he always had a cheery smile and a kind word for everyone. He was made welcome wherever he went.

Inevitably the time came when Frewin bought a motor vehicle, and this reduced the number of his working hours considerably. He always maintained though, that his happiest recollections of his life on the road were when he was driving home in his covered van, pulled by his beloved horse 'Jack', in the light of the full moon, known to country folk as the 'Parish Lantern'. – *Kathleen Burton*

**Frewin Gray with his beloved horse 'Jack'**

# A Hallowe'en Visit to Dracula's Den

*Derek MacKenzie Hook*

ALMOST constantly shrouded in sea mist, the spectral outlines of Slains Castle dominate the coastline above Cruden Bay. It would take a brave person to venture into the depths of this haunting ruin after sunset, but for Bram Stoker it was not the witches of Hallowe'en that lurked in the bowels of Slains Castle, but the servants of the Prince of Darkness himself, Count Dracula.

Hallowe'en, or All Hallows' Eve (31 October), appears in the Christian Calendar at the festival of All Saints, which commemorates the 'blessed dead' who have been canonised. It was the policy of the early Christian Church to graft a Christian festival upon each pagan one in order to disrupt the customs of the people as little as possible, so they grafted Hallowe'en upon the ancient Celtic festival of Samhuinn, which marked the entry of the Celtic year.

The Celts bisected the year at Beltane (1 May) and Samhuinn (1 November), to mark the entry of summer and winter, with festivals beginning on their eve. This division being a natural progression in a period at a pastoral stage of development, the flocks and herds going out to their summer pastures at Beltane and returning to the fold at Samhuinn. A blessing was invoked upon hunter, herdsman, stock and crops at Beltane, whilst Samhuinn was a day of thanksgiving for the supply of food and safe return of the stockmen.

Hallowe'en was also the date of a great witches' 'Sabbath' or conventicle. Witches and warlocks, it was said, might be seen after dark cleaving the air on broomsticks on their way to the Hallowmas Rade. As a festival of beginnings, the ancient Samhuinn was accompanied with orgiastic rites and these continued to be practised by followers of the witch cult on Hallowe'en.

So to explore this enigmatic site that stirs the memories of one of the most horrific tales in English Literature... Through a maze of passageways and chambers lies a dark, underground vault. Strike a match and discover huge stone slabs resting at odd angles. Could this have been the crypt? Perhaps it is more likely to have been the wine cellar. Best to move swiftly on through Slains labyrinth of ruinous corridors and chasms. Pause for a moment to gaze

# SUBSCRIPTION AND ENROLMENT FORMS

## FOR ALL SUBSCRIBERS AND MEMBERS

Mr/Mrs/Miss .............................................................................................................................

Please use CAPITAL LETTERS

Address ...................................................................................................................................

...................................................................................................................................

................................................................................. Postcode ...........................................

I would like to pay by: (Please tick one box only but be sure to give your full details)

☐ **A. DEBIT/CREDIT CARD** (Switch, Visa, Access/Mastercard or Amex)

I authorise you to debit my debit/credit card with the annual subscription on receipt and annually thereafter on the same date unless cancelled by me.

1. Please tick box ☐ Switch ☐ Visa ☐ Access/Mastercard ☐ Amex

2. Card No ☐☐☐☐☐☐☐☐☐☐☐☐☐☐☐☐

3. Expiry date ☐☐ — ☐☐

4. Signed ................................................................ Date ...........................................

☐ **B. DIRECT DEBIT**

**DIRECT Debit**

Payment instruction to Bank/Building Society Originator's Identification No: 930895

1. To the Manager ...............................................................................................................

........................................................................................Bank/Building Society

2. Account in the Name of ...................................................................................................

3. Account No ☐☐☐☐☐☐☐☐  Sort code ☐☐ — ☐☐ — ☐☐

4. Instruction to Bank/Building Society

Please pay The Countrylover's Club Direct Debits from the account detailed on this Instruction subject to the safeguards assured by The Direct Debit Guarantee.

5. Signed ................................................................ Date ...........................................

☐ **C. CASH**

## SUBSCRIPTION TO COUNTRY ORIGINS

|  |  | UK | Europe | ROW |
|---|---|---|---|---|
| A/B | ☐ Country Origins by Debit/Credit Card or Direct Debit | £9.90 | £12.78 | £17.00 |
| C | ☐ Country Origins by cash | £11.00 | £14.20 | £19.00 |

You May Of Course Cancel At Any Time
Return completed form to:
THE COUNTRYLOVER'S CLUB, PO Box 4, Nairn IV12 4HU

CO/5/96

# THE DAVID THOMAS CHARITABLE TRUST AWARDS

**NEW**

## HARVEST MEMORIES
## ENTRY FORM

(Mr/Mrs/Miss) ........................................................................................

Address ...............................................................................................

.............................................. Postcode .........................................

I would like to enter the Harvest Memories competition whose rules are printed on the competition page of the current issue of *Country Origins* and agree to be bound by the rules set out there. Entry fees are £2.50 minimum (£3.50 preferred, £5.00 welcome to assist the work of the DT Charitable Trust). I enclose:

a) my story titled ..................................................... b) my entry fee £ .....................

Please make cheques/postal orders payable to the David Thomas Charitable Trust.
Or if you prefer: Switch/Visa/Access/Amex (delete as appropriate) Amount £ ☐

Card No ☐☐☐☐☐☐☐☐☐☐☐☐☐☐☐☐ Expiry ☐☐☐☐

Signed ...............................................................................................

Note entries must be postmarked by 30 March 1997

---

**STILL TIME TO ENTER**

## MARKET DAY MEMORIES
## ENTRY FORM

(Mr/Mrs/Miss) ........................................................................................

Address ...............................................................................................

.............................................. Postcode .........................................

I would like to enter the Market Day Memories competition whose rules are printed on the competition page of the current issue of *Country Origins* and agree to be bound by the rules set out there. Entry fees are £2.50 minimum (£3.50 preferred, £5.00 welcome to assist the work of the DT Charitable Trust). I enclose:

a) my story titled ..................................................... b) my entry fee £ .....................

Please make cheques/postal orders payable to the David Thomas Charitable Trust.
Or if you prefer: Switch/Visa/Access/Amex (delete as appropriate) Amount £ ☐

Card No ☐☐☐☐☐☐☐☐☐☐☐☐☐☐☐☐ Expiry ☐☐☐☐

Signed ...............................................................................................

Note entries must be postmarked by 31 December 1996

---

# TO YOUR NEWSAGENT

Please order me a copy of the quarterly *Country Origins*.
Next issue on sale 8 November 1996.

Name ...............................................................................................

Address ...............................................................................................

.............................................. Postcode .........................................

across the bay where a rocky outcrop known as the Skares protrude perilously into the sea, treacherous rocks that have claimed the lives of many seamen over the centuries. This was Stoker's favourite haunt: he based his novel, *Mysteries of the Sea* on the legends of the Skares and it is said that in the light of the full moon of the Lammas tide victims claimed by the killer rocks emerge from the sea; '*Up the steep path came a silent procession of ghostly figures, so misty of outline that through the grey-green of their phantom beings the rocks and moonlit sea were apparent.*'

In the lengthening shadows from the rapidly setting sun and ever dwindling light, it is easy for the eyes to play tricks and fuel the imagination even further. Safer to head for the village and the local hostelry.

It was in this very hotel that Bram Stoker himself once stayed. He wrote in the visitors book '*delighted with everything and everybody – hope to come again*'.

Legend would have us believe that this was the setting that inspired Bram Stoker to write his Gothic chiller whilst visiting this wild stretch of Buchan coast in 1893. Early drafts of the story had the evil Count coming ashore here, although this was later changed to Whitby in Yorkshire.

When the North Sea haar has lifted, Slains is a fine ruin. First erected in 1597 by the 9th Earl of Errol, it was then rebuilt and added to by subsequent Earls, the last great reconstruction being made in 1837. It was in 1773 that Johnson and Boswell visited Slains during their travels and

**Slains Castle**

described how, '*the walls of one of the towers seem only a continuation of the perpendicular rock, the foot of which is beaten by the waves*'. Boswell was not too impressed with the hospitality shown by the Earl of Errol and complained, '*the sea to which my window looked, roared, and the pillows were made of some sea-fowl's feathers which had to me a disagreeable smell*'.

It was during the time of the 19th Earl that the Castle enjoyed its greatest days when playing host to many notable actors and artistes of the era. Bram Stoker was a regular guest during this time. When the 20th Earl was forced to sell the Castle in 1916 to pay death duties, the deterioration of the building was swift. The new owner allowed it to fall into a state of disrepair, having the roof removed in 1925 and the Castle partially dismantled.

Cruden Bay itself, with its two mile crescent of flat, golden sands, is a fine resort. The name of Cruden was derived from '*croju-dane*', meaning '*slaughter of the Danes*'. It was here in 1012 that King Malcolm II of Scotland won a bloody battle against Canute and his Danish army, a font in the nearby St James' Church of Cruden is said to have originated from a church built by Malcolm II on the battlefield to mark his victory.

It was from the sands of Cruden Bay on 30 July, 1914 that a single seater plane with Norwegian, pilot Commander Tryggve Gran made the first ever flight across the North Sea – 300 miles to Stavanger in Norway.

Perched precariously on the cliff tops nearby is the tiny community of Bullers O' Buchan. In 1881 it was a thriving fishing community, supporting 21 fishing boats and 43 fishermen. Today it is purely residential, enduring an isolated charm, its only companion being the sea and the colony of gulls that raucously circulate the natural amphitheatre of the nearby Bullers. This was once a massive cave until the roof collapsed and created this 200ft deep, sea-chasm. A spectacular sight, the water roars in at sea level through a narrow rock archway, hence its name 'Bullers', or boilers. When visiting with Johnson in 1883, James Boswell aptly described it as a '*monstrous caldron*'.

This coastline is a seabird's paradise and supports breeding colonies of kittiwake, razorbill, shag, guillemot, fulmar, and herring gull; its natural auditorium providing a stage for the chorus from a variety of birds. When visiting the Buchan coast, T.E. Lawrence defined the phenomenon as, '*the saddest, most cold, disembodied voices in the world*'.

**Cruden Bay is located on the A975, 24 miles north of Aberdeen.**

*For further information contact:*
*Grampian, Highlands & Aberdeen*
*Tourism Marketing Company,*
*St Nicholas House,*
*Broad Street,*
*Aberdeen AB9 1DE*
*Tel: 01224 632727*

*Banff and Buchan Tourist Board,*
*Collie Lodge,*
*Banff AB45 1AU*
*Tel: 01261 812789*

*Opposite:* **Bullers of Buchan**

# Fiery Fluid

## *Jerome Betts*

IN the past, the number of people killed or injured by what Benjamin Franklin called 'the electrical fluid' was much greater than today. According to Professor D.M. Elsom of the Tornado and Storm Research Organisation (TORRO) at Oxford Brookes University, there were well over forty deaths in the United Kingdom for the years 1852, 1872 and 1895.

Since 1960, in contrast, there have been only two years when the number of deaths has exceeded ten. Among the reasons for the decline is the mechanization of agriculture, farm-labourers at work in the fields forming the largest group of victims in former centuries.

Back in 1718, two such workers, John Hewet and Sarah Drew, killed instantly by lightning on the last day of July while harvesting with others at Stanton Harcourt in Oxfordshire, managed to achieve a minor niche in literary history. They were provided with an epitaph by the poet Alexander Pope, who had chanced to arrive to stay nearby on the evening of their funeral and was touched by the fate of the two young village sweethearts, who had been preparing to marry.

Pope's friend Lord Harcourt paid for a memorial stone still set in the exterior wall of the South transept of Saint Michael's Church Stanton Harcourt. The inscription combines a plain prose account of the tragedy with verses by Pope stressing the couple's blameless lives. The first four lines were directed especially at some of the villagers who, in the days before the forces at work were understood, saw the manner of John and Sarah's death as implying divine retribution, and were disturbed by their being allowed Christian burial together in the churchyard.

*Think not by rigorous judgment seiz'd,*
  *A Pair so faithful could expire;*
*Victims so pure Heav'n saw well pleas'd,*
  *And snatch'd them in caelestial fire.*

*Live well & fear no sudden fate:*
  *When God calls Virtue to the grave,*
*Alike 'tis Justice soon or late,*
  *Mercy alike to kill or save.*

*Virtue unmov'd can hear the Call,*
*And face the Flash that melts the Ball.*

The expansion of built-up areas in our times also means that there are more structures — whether or not equipped with Benjamin Franklin's invention — to divert lightning away from people, and there is likewise increased awareness of the need for precautions during thunderstorms.

Another factor is the improvement in emergency medical treatment. The spread of knowledge about external cardiac massage and mouth-to-mouth techniques has facilitated the prompt resuscitation so vital for lightning victims like the unfortunate John and Sarah.

Anything that brings human beings into the fields and open spaces again will restore the risk. Not surprisingly, many reports of lightning injuries are these days connected with people engaged in outdoor recreation rather than rural labour. A schoolteacher, for example, was killed as he led a party in Snowdonia in May 1981, and on 24 July, 1994 – a day on which the Electrical Association's lightning-location system registered over 82,000 ground-strokes and two Welsh oil-refineries went up in flames – a young man walking on the Stiperstones near Shrewsbury became one of the five people to be killed by lightning in the UK in 1994.

In fact, 1994 saw a rise in the number of deaths due to lightning compared with some previous years. 1987 and 1990 had only one fatality each. TORRO's records of incidents for 1975–93 suggest that the average annual number of people struck by lightning in the UK is 24, of whom four will die.

Such an average, of course, conceals wide fluctuations, as when an entire group is affected by an adjacent strike. Something like this happened during a storm at Crewkerne Somerset in 1983, when school hockey players were hit by a solitary flash, one of them later dying of the injuries received.

When once, in the era of a thickly-populated working countryside, mowers and harvesters used to swing their scythes and hooks, members now often swing their clubs. In electrical storms, golf-courses have a potentially lethal mixture of open spaces and trees, as well as the metal clubs and metal-tipped umbrellas that project invitingly above human heads. Lightning – either in the form of direct strikes, side-flash from trees, contact-voltage transmitted between huddled players, and step-voltage from nearby ground impacts – thus takes a relatively high toll of golfers.

One such striking event, fortunately not fatal, occurred during the Church in Wales Clergy Golf Championship at Builth Wells in June 1993. The umbrella being held by the Reverend Keith Davies was hit by lightning as the eighteen clerical competitors ran for cover when a storm broke. Sparks and smoke flew from the handle, but Mr Davies was not harmed, if somewhat shaken. Clearly both the wet and fiery kinds of fluid fall on all alike, and the bolt is no respecter of the cloth.

*Golf-course Bangor North Wales.* **Lightning can be a hazard on mountains and golf-courses, particularly with the proximity of tall solitary trees.**

John Rocha

## COMPETITIONS

# £250 for your harvest memories

Do you remember the good old fashioned harvest days, when everyone in the village lent a hand to bring the harvest home... and when everyone danced the night away at the harvest supper – but was still there for a good, rousing harvest festival service at the village church? Can you capture the spirit of those days, and capture them in words? If so, here is a writing competition with a chance to win a first prize of £250 or one of the two runners-up prizes of £50 each. Entries should be up to 500 words, and closing date is 30 March 1997. Full rules are set out on the opposite page.

Norman Duerden

## STILL TIME TO ENTER

# £250 for your market day memories

Do you remember market days as they used to be in country towns? The days when local farmers brought their livestock into town, when the fruit and vegetable stalls sold produce straight from the nearby farms, when thrifty housewives did the shopping for the week? If you can recall those days, here is your chance to write about them and perhaps to win the first prize of £250 or one of the two runners-up prizes of £50 each. Closing date is 31 December 1996, full rules on the opposite page.

Editor's advice: When writing about your memories, either for the harvest memories or the market day memories competition, try to act as a reporter rather than using the first-person I and putting yourself too strongly in the frame. And if you can enclose any photographs with your entry, that would certainly enhance your chance of winning.

## Competition rules

1. To enter. Entrants must be over 16 years of age at the time of entry and must not have earned an aggregate of more than £10,000 from their writing in the last ten years. Employees of Writers News Limited and regular contributors to magazines published by Writers News Limited are not eligible to enter either competition.

2. Entries. Manuscripts should be typed in double spacing on single sides of A4 paper, and should be fronted by a title page stating the competition for which the entry is intended, the entrant's name and address and (if possible) a daytime telephone number. The title page should also state whether any photographs accompany the manuscript, and if so how many. Photographs should carry a label on their reverse stating the name and address of the entrant.

Entries must be original material not previously submitted for publication nor currently submitted to any other competition (nor will they be so submitted before the date given in rule 7).

3. Harvest Memories: Entries should be posted to Competition Department (Harvest Memories), The Countrylover's Club, PO Box 4, Nairn IV12 4HU and must be postmarked by 30 March 97. Market Day Memories: Entries should be posted to Competition Department (Market Memories), The Countrylover's Club, PO Box 4, Nairn IV12 4HU and must be postmarked by 31 December 1996. Entries cannot be accepted by fax, and proof of posting cannot be accepted as proof of delivery.

4. Manuscripts will be returned if accompanied by a stamped and addressed envelope. If you wish receipt of your entry to be acknowledged, please enclose a suitably worded stamped and self-addressed postcard. Whilst every care will be taken with manuscripts and photographs, the competition organisers cannot be responsible for lost, damaged or delayed material.

5. Entries must be accompanied by a copy of the entry form (see card opposite page 115) together with the entry fee. Entry fee for each competition is £2.50 minimum; £3.50 is the preferred fee, whilst £5 would

be welcome to assist with the work of the DT Charitable Trust. You can help yourself (and us) by purchasing entry coupons for four competitions (or three entry coupons if your purchase order accompanies your entry to a competition). £10 is the minimum amount to purchase you entry coupons; £14 is the preferred fee, whilst £20 would be welcome to assist with the work of the DT Charitable Trust. Payment for a set of four entries may be made by Visa or Mastercard. All payments should be made to the DT Charitable Trust.

Because of high bank charges, overseas currency is not accepted and overseas entrants are therefore advised to purchase entry coupons (alternatively, please send six International Reply Coupons as entry fee for any single competition).

6. Judging: Competitions will be judged by persons appointed by the agents of the David Thomas Charitable Trust, and the decision of the judges will be final and no correspondence or discussion will be entered into.

7. Harvest Memories: A first prize of £250 will be awarded together with two runners-up awards of £50 each. Winners will be notified by 20 May 1997 and the winning entry will be published in the Autumn 1997 issue of *Country Origins*. Market Day Memories: A first prize of £250 will be awarded together with two runners-up awards of £50 each. Winners will be notified by 20 February 1997 and the winning entry will be published in the Summer 1997 issue of *Country Origins*. Entries may be submitted for publication elsewhere after the given notification dates.

8. The trustees of the David Thomas Charitable Trust retains the right to publish (in full or abridged) winning and runners-up entries in any book, magazine or publication issues by or associated with Writers News Limited without further payment. Entrants undertake not to make any other use of winning or runners-up entries for eighteen months after the announcement of results without written permission. Copyright remains vested with the writer.

## REFLECTIONS

# Wartime Memories

### Neutrality

IN wartime Dublin there was a shortage of mustard. This was serious as visitors to the neutral capital looked forward to their unrationed steak. Cream cakes were much in demand, and Alka-seltzer. Sales of Guinness and John Jameson were high. (When George IV visited in 1821 he is said to have left in a slightly inebriated state.)

The war years brought no blackout to Southern Irish cities. The mail-boat, sliding in to Kingstown harbour in the early morning, was embraced by the twin piers with their

**'Kingstown', now Dun Laoghaire, from the pier**

twinkling lights, bringing a lump to the throats of service-men returning home on leave.

They were forbidden to land in uniform although a greater proportion of the population from the South than the North volunteered to fight. Many of the Generals were Irish – Alexander Auchinlech, Montgomery. It is only now, fifty years on, that a service of commemoration has been held for those who gave their lives in battle.

The frontier with Northern Ireland, on the railway, was at Goraghwood. Customs officials would board the train and school-girls, returning after the holidays, would have to open their trunks from the luggage-van. Chief among the items of contraband were French lipsticks and soap,

DUN LAOGHAIRE FROM THE PIER.                                        R 1691

silk stockings, chocolate and sweets. There was speculation as to whether a lacrosse stick was a weapon of war, for firing a sling-shot, or was truly, as was claimed, for playing a game. The whole performance seemed somewhat farcical.

Coal was in short supply and trains, travelling South to Cork or West to Galway, were cold and very late. Sometimes they were stranded deep in the country and the crew had to resort to pulling out fencing-posts to get up steam.

The equivalent of 'Dad's Army' was the Local Defence Force, or L.D.F. They roamed the fields armed only with binoculars, searching for parachutists who might belong to either side. Luckily few were spotted. Stray bombs fell on creameries or cow-sheds, dropped by planes lost, or lightening their load, on the way home from raids on Liverpool or Bristol. They rattled the silver on the ancient sideboards of country houses.

West of the River Shannon, where memories of the potato famine and harsh absentee landlords lingered amongst the poor, Germany seemed to offer a new beginning. Lord Haw-haw was listened to here with more credulity than in the more affluent Eastern Counties. There was said to be a German submarine lurking in Galway Bay. Perhaps the crew had discovered that lobsters could be had fresh from the sea, for the price of half-a-crown! Certain German Embassy staff walked the cliff tops with maps and cameras, and after the war many German families bought properties in Eire. Few of them are still there, whereas Kinsale, in West Cork, is known locally as 'Little England'. – *Hetty Staples*

---

## Waste not, want not

IN July 1940 with the Battle of Britain raging, mother won her own small but important victory. She perfected a method of making a spread for bread go a long way, necessary since the combined ration was eight ounces of butter, margarine and cooking fat per person.

She took the yellow butter from the greaseproof paper in which the grocer had cut, weighed and wrapped it, and put it into a china bowl, its exterior bedecked with honey-coloured relief patterns. The cream-coloured margarine often came in the manufacturer's wrapper, and scraping both slightly warmed papers with a knife was obligatory. So that not a smear was wasted the papers were rubbed round the frying pan, and then kept as firelighters.

The bowl went into warm water for twenty minutes, essential because butter was soft and margarine was hard, and without the mellowness induced by warmth they would never combine. In a separate dish she had a measured amount of flour which was warmed to the same temperature.

As the fat mixture softened she took the horizontally banded blue and white china jug from the warm water and removed the calico cover, which kept flies out of the milk. It had triangular lace tassels round its edge weighted with assorted coloured glass beads which kept it taut and stopped it from falling in. Children through it beautiful and sister Barbara sometimes put it on her head and surveyed herself in the looking glass.

Mother poured a little of the milk into the mix with a sprinkling of flour and continued to stir with the worn tablespoon which had belonged to her mother-in-law. The hand-operated whisk had caused separation and she knew that if milk was added too quickly it would happen again. Little by little the remaining ingredients were carefully incorporated.

The result was a finely balanced emulsion, soft and buttery, which fitted well into her thrifty, scrape-it-on-and-scrape-it-off philosophy, learned in the hard times of peace and now useful in the even harder times of war. She had increased the volume of the ration by about fifteen percent and we rejoiced in her success.

In the beginning, there were some disasters when the mix separated because of too much milk or not enough even warmth. Then she poured off the liquid and we had to make the best of a sloppy mess. But it did not take her long to reach the time when it came right every week, even when she included the flour. We applauded her triumph, for it meant that we could have 'butter' on our bread, something we had not always achieved in peace time.

Her other great success was in ren-

**Mother in 1943 with Mephistopheles the cat and her husband, Billy Reed**

dering fat off meat. She cut it in half inch pieces and placed it in a saucepan on the yellow flame paraffin stove or the blue flame Primus. It had to be watched, for it spat and took fire easily. Sometimes the result was used for cooking, while at others it was delicious dripping to be spread on our bread with salt and pepper in order to save the 'butter'. The crinkled brown bits left in the saucepan we ate like the pork scratchings sold today. – *Frank Reed*

## Night invasion

EARLY in the spring of 1944 preparations were in hand for the invasion of France. Of course, very few people knew the details or even the rough plan, but there was a feeling abroad in the country that 'something big' was coming up. Joan was in a better position than most to appreciate what was going on. The cottage she rented lay just to the east of the Burseldon Bridge over the Hamble River. Today this is a colourful and busy yacht haven, but in 1944 it was very different. The whole area had been bombed steadily during the previous four years, and the toll of makeshift repairs and demolition had rendered the area desolate.

The roads and lanes around Hamble were filling with every type of military hardware. Lorries, trailers, guns, tanks, ambulances, and some structures that no-one could even guess the purpose of. Joan was used to seeing convoys of equipment pass through on their way to the docks at Southampton, but this was different. The sheer scale of the build-up was staggering. Long rows of jeeps were parked along the verges of back lanes, carefully covered with camouflage netting.

One night, Joan was sitting by the fire knitting and listening to the radio. Her social life took place during the day, with the other young women who lived nearby. All of a sudden there came a knock at the door. Joan was surprised, but not alarmed. Probably Betty from next door, run out of wool or something. She switched off the living room light (the door opened directly on to the lane) and opened the door. By the flickering light of the fire she saw the figure of a man looming above her. White teeth suddenly flashed a grin in a blackened face. Little wisps of twig twitched and fluttered in his helmet. 'May we come in, Mam?' said an American accent. We? thought Joan. In they came – six of them, all dressed in full combat gear, all with blackened faces, all looking excited, nervous and about seventeen years old. Joan had no idea what they wanted, who they were, or indeed what to do, so she fell back on the old English standby: 'Would you boys like a cup of tea?'

The night passed quietly enough. The lads told her a little bit about themselves (no details of what they were doing, of course), and were obviously delighted at being entertained by such an attractive young woman. At around four in the morn-ing they said their goodbyes, and slipped out of the back door and into the dawn. Joan never saw them again.

Two days later, every engine in every truck, tank, self-propelled gun – indeed every vehicle for miles around – came to life. Thousands of men appeared from nowhere; for two days the engines roared and the convoys slowly rumbled past Meadow Cottage, heading towards the Hamble and Southampton.

On the third morning, the roads were empty. Just churned-up verges and a lingering smell of petrol. Not quiet, however, for overhead there was an endless stream of aircraft, all heading in the one direction – to France. By that afternoon on the radio the news was out – the invasion of France had started. Many excited and upbeat messages were being given out, about the success of the landings and the lighter than expect-ed casualties.

But one bit of news made Joan sit up and pay extra attention. It con-cerned the Special Forces who had gone in two or three days early, to prepare the way for the landings by sabotaging the German defences along the coast of France. These men had secretly made their way into the very teeth of the defences, without recognition or assistance from the forces in England for fear of breaking the secrecy and exposing the invasion plan.

Men? thought Joan. They were just boys, just young lads so grateful for some warmth, tea and cakes from a woman living in a little cottage on their path to war. – *Roger C. Tindley*

# How to Trace Your Family Tree

## The Village School

MOST of our ancestors who attended school in the last 100 years attended elementary schools (now primary schools). A number of these schools' histories will go back over 400 years although records are only usually found from the 19th century onwards.

From a Family History point of view 1833 became a turning point in record keeping as from this date the state started to give financial aid to the church schools and in the 1850s accountability was being asked for. A system in 1862 was brought in force called 'payment by results' which was designed to make education either cheaper or more efficient but what it did do was make each school keep better and more accurate records, as the teacher's salary depended on it.

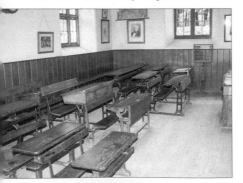

Because of this, more information on each child was starting to be kept including names and addresses, dates of birth, and names of parents.

*Background*
Education in one form or another has been around since the late 6th century, and as with many aspects of our life the church has played a significant role. In 1120 a rector in a village in Leicester started a school for local boys 'to keep them out of mischief'.

If no building was available in the local community to be used as a school then the church itself was used, especially if the priest was the teacher, which was highly likely as to be a teacher/schoolmaster you had to be approved by the Bishop of the Diocese. Even today you will see on some church walls around the country signs of their uses as visual aids by having multiplication tables or the alphabet printed on them.

*School Attendance*
School attendance by the pupils was erratic especially in the rural districts when their services were required to help out on the land. For the country child, schools were not usually in every community and some children

could walk up to two miles to get to school and two miles back home again. Although school tended to run from 9am to 4pm in the summer and to 3.30pm in winter, they were usually also required to carry out chores before and after school for their family so their day was long. Attendance was always affected by the needs of the children on the land.

Various systems and acts of parliament were introduced to try to encourage and sometimes force children to school. One of these inducements was introduced in 1853 for the agricultural districts and was known as Capitation Grants. These grants worked on paying the school between 4s and 6s for a boy and 3s to 5s per girl if they had attended school for at least 176 days of the year. Various education acts between 1870 and 1880 made school for the over fives compulsory. However more often than not if a child did not attend action was not taken as it was felt that their contribution at harvest time was more important.

There was a special act brought in in 1875 to cope with the needs of the rural children called the Agricultural Children's Act. This stated that children under eight should not work. Between eight and ten they could only work if they had made 250 attendances at school and between ten and twelve the minimum was 150 attendances. Short term measures to cope with the harvesting needs allowed certain exemptions to take place during hay, corn or hop harvests. At other times of the year farmers had to apply to the local magistrates for exemption certificates for specific

children. These records can be found amongst the Local Petty Session records in the relevant county record office.

Of course not going to school, up to 1891, was not always because of work. Other factors included the weather; ill health; shoes (children had to wear shoes to school, and when a farm worker was only receiving 10s to 14s a week for his labour and shoes cost 8s a pair, most families couldn't afford this luxury); living more than two miles from the school; family circumstances (needing to look after younger members of the family); and the school fees (1d to 2d a week per child) could not be met, especially if more than one child was at school; could all be reasons for not attending. In 1891 school fees for elementary education were abolished. Truancy amongst the children for their own reasons also happened. In one particular case a young lad had truanted from a school a number of times so on one occasion his mother took him to school and strapped him (using rope) to the gallery to make sure he stayed put. His determination not to be at school however, meant that by dinner time that day he had bitten through the rope and disappeared again.

The low attendance at school for certain periods of the year led to the timing of school holidays being changed to cope with the needs of the community. In rural areas this meant that the holidays would coincide with the harvesting periods, so the children could be used on the farms without affecting their school attendance.

Many schools tried introducing various methods to encourage and therefore reward the children for attending school. Such items as banners, gifts and other inducements were used. Not usually money, except in some schools on limited occasions.

*School Dinners*
School meals prior to the Education Act of 1906 were not universally provided. In the rural areas children would take their lunch with them which consisted of bread and lard. Some areas would produce hot soup in the winter for two days a week, and by 1876 some schools provided hot 'penny dinners' during the winter months although these were restricted to those who could afford them. Some children from the wealthier families would bring in bread and would be allowed to toast it using the school fire. In some schools special stools were provided by the fire for this purpose.

Lunch breaks were usually two hours long, particularly in summer, and once the meal was eaten the children were allowed to play outside, paddle in the nearby stream, playing chase and ball games in the nearby fields, and some children would chase the cows.

In 1906 the education act included provision that required the local authorities to provide school meals for the children. This became fully established during World War 2.

A special act called the Milk in Schools Act was introduced in 1934, and this provided for milk to be given to the children although until 1946 there was a small charge. In 1946, a change in the law meant that the milk should be provided free of charge. Records relating to this set of school services can be found in the Public Record Office in London.

*The Village Schoolmaster*
The villages of yesteryear were very different to that of today. Many people within the community gained their income from the land in one form or another, and the schoolmaster was no exception.

If a village was lucky enough to have a schoolmaster he was considered a village officer and would be paid partly in fees, partly from an endowment of land, and very often would supplement this income by doing farming in his spare time, plus occasionally some book-keeping, will writing, land surveying and appraising. A very busy person indeed. In short all the villagers were a close knit community.

*What They Learned*

Up to the 1860s the primary task of most of the schools set up was to teach its pupils the 3 Rs. Reading was achieved by the rote system, which used a method of repetitive teaching and 'off by heart' method, usually using the bible as this was sometimes the only book the school would have.

Writing was carried out on slates using a slate pencil as these could be cleaned, usually by the children themselves and most likely with spit and using their sleeves. They were first taught to command the 'pot hooks' and then this would lead into 'letters'. They would then have to copy these continually until they had improved and mastered each letter. This would then lead on to dictation. In arithmetic they would stick to the basics of adding, subtracting, dividing and multiplying.

If the class consisted of many children at different levels, as it did in many cases, then those children that were able would be given long complicated tasks to carry out to keep them occupied while the teacher concentrated on the others. The type of task they would be given, which in many cases would keep them going all day, would be: '*How many furlongs, rods, yards, feet and inches, and barleycorns will reach around the earth assuming it to be 25,020 miles to best calculation?*' Other lessons that would also be undertaken in some schools included singing, religious instruction and needlework.

Over time as various Education Acts were introduced so were other subjects for the pupils, usually with the bribe of a grant. For example in 1867 grant aid was introduced for history, geography and grammar and it was hoped this would improve the curriculum. Then in 1870 drawing was added. These tasks were not compulsory but if not carried out then these specific grants would not be available to the school. By 1890 drawing became a compulsory activity for boys.

*What Records Can We Find?*

The types of records produced and kept by the schools would include; admission registers, log books, examination and assessment records, absenteeism books, punishment books, medals and honours, leaving certificates, school magazines, photographs and many more. Some, many or all can be kept, but it will differ from school to school and sometimes it will depend on the diligence of the school head. These can now be found either with the county education authority, county records office, libraries, museums or even still with the school if it still exists. Hunt around.

# Petersfield Physic Garden

*Patricia Cleveland-Peck*

IN the country town of Petersfield, Hampshire, tucked away behind the High Street, there is a delightful garden. It is a new garden created in the style of the 17th century 'Physic' or herb gardens but in fact it celebrates an even older link with gardening for records show that the land on which it is situated was a 12th century burage plot, or allotment which means that the ground has been gardened continuously for eight centuries.

The Hampshire Garden Trust acquired this valuable site a few years ago through the generosity of a local man, a Major J.C.E. Bowen, whose orchard and vegetable garden it had been. Major Bowen was a conservationist and traveller, the third generation of an Indian Army family. Sadly he did not live to see the garden finished but as a memorial to him a sundial has been erected in the garden. As, during his extensive travels he studied the Persian poets, a verse from his translation of Amir Khusru, a poet who died in 1324, has been engraved around the dial, providing yet another connection between the Middle Ages and this little garden:

*Within this scented garden close*
*Whose desires may bring repose*
*An earthly Paradise it seems –*
*Of cypresses, green lawns, and streams –*
*And if your host you wish to please*
*Converse of nothing else but these...*

Major Bowen left the land to be held in trust for the education and enjoyment of the public and now it is well on the way to being a small earthly paradise. However, originally the only assets were the exceptionally good soil (quantities of oyster shell, in previous centuries a food of the poor, were discovered) and the old orchard. This included a magnificently gnarled specimen of the old Hampshire apple, Hambleton Deux Ans, so called because of it would keep for two years.

Since then, to maintain the 17th century theme, a topiary walk has been laid out, a yew hedge planted and a small orchard of old fruit varieties established. These include Nonpareil, Margil and Court Pendu Plat apples, Carillac pear, Medlar, Quince, Shropshire Prune Damson, apricots, figs and vines. Box clipped into cones and pyramids are already doing well and old roses like La Belle

# Complete your set of Country Origins

Already many readers say that they'll build up a complete set of *Country Origins*. Each issue carries a small number at the foot of its spine to make collection easy and rewarding. If you missed the first issue, why not send £2.95 for a copy now (£5 (post free) for issues one and two, £7.50 (post free) for issues one, two and three, £10 (post free) for issues one, two, three and four)... and do either take out a postal subscription to ensure you receive each issue on the day of publication or place a regular order with your newsagent.

And of course show the magazine to the kind of people likely to be interested in it. Out there are thousands of people who will surely fall in love with as much as the first readers, like LJP of Camborne, Cornwall, who says: 'Excellent. Don't change this format. It is just the right size and content mix.'

**Send to: Back Issues,
The Countrylover's Club,
PO Box 4, Nairn IV12 4HU**

# *Recommend a Friend...*

Know Someone Who Would Benefit From COUNTRY ORIGINS?
Just think of all your friends who would be interested in reading *Country Origins*. Send us their names... we will send them details (without mentioning your name) – and each time one of them becomes a subscriber you will receive a £10 voucher.

Please send details of COUNTRY ORIGINS to: (*Names and addresses in* CAPITALS *please*)

Name ............................................................ Address ............................................................

......................................................................................... Postcode ............................

Name ............................................................ Address ............................................................

......................................................................................... Postcode ............................

Name ............................................................Address ............................................................

......................................................................................... Postcode ............................

*(Any further names and address may be writtenn on a separate piece of paper and attached to this form)*

MY OWN DETAILS ARE:

Subscription No ............................................... Name ............................................................

Address ...................................................................................................................................

......................................................................................... Postcode ............................

CO/5/96

**To: THE COUNTRYLOVER'S CLUB, PO BOX 4, NAIRN IV12 4HU**

# GIFT SUBSCRIPTION OFFER

Your gift problems solved!
From only £14.25 you can make a gift guaranteed to give year-round pleasure
*Country Origins* and **The Countrylover's Calendar 1997.**
And for every two such gift subscriptions you make we will send you, the donor,
a **FREE** The Countrylover's Calendar 1997 (as soon as it is available).

## GIFT SUBSCRIPTION APPLICATION FORM

My name ..................................................................................................................

My address ..............................................................................................................

.................................................................................. Postcode ...............................

I would like the following gift membership/subscription to be despatched to the Nominated Gift
Subscriber below.

| *Please tick as appropriate* | UK | *Europe/Eire and ROW†* *by surface* | *Outside Europe* *by air* |
|---|---|---|---|
| **Country Origins** and Calendar | £14.25 ☐ | £17.50 ☐ | £18.50 ☐ |

† *ROW* – Rest of the world

## NOMINATED GIFT SUBSCRIBER ONE

Name .......................................................................................................................

Address ...................................................................................................................

.................................................................................. Postcode ...............................

## NOMINATED GIFT SUBSCRIBER TWO

Name .......................................................................................................................

Address ...................................................................................................................

.................................................................................. Postcode ...............................

## NOMINATED GIFT SUBSCRIBER THREE

Name .......................................................................................................................

Address ...................................................................................................................

.................................................................................. Postcode ...............................

## PAYMENT

Total amount of all items ordered: £ [          ]

I prefer to pay by debit/credit card/cheque/postal order and will pay for one year gift subscription for
each of the above.

☐ **DEBIT/CREDIT CARD** (Switch, Visa, Access/Mastercard or Amex)

I authorise you to debit my debit/credit card with the gift subscription unless cancelled by me.

1. Please tick    Switch ☐    Visa ☐    Access/Mastercard ☐    Amex ☐

2. Card No [ ][ ][ ][ ][ ][ ][ ][ ][ ][ ][ ][ ][ ][ ][ ][ ]    3. Expiry date [  ] — [  ]

4. Signed ............................................................................ Date ...............................

☐ **CASH**

1. I send cheque/postal order made out to *The Countrylover's Club* for £ [          ]

Please return to THE COUNTRYLOVER'S CLUB, PO Box 4, Nairn IV12 4HU    CO/5/96

Distinguée and rosa Hemisphaerica enjoy the shelter of the mellow walls. A bed of 'Florist's Flowers' remind us of the amazing varieties which 17th century gardeners grew.

A competition was held to design a knot garden and the winning knot, by Mrs Joanne Allen, has been planted up and is now maturing well. Herbaceous plants including old pinks, Cheiranthus Bloody Warrior and Harpur Crewe, auriculas, Hose-in-hose and Jack in the Green primroses, Lobelia syphilitica (the old remedy for syphilis) tulips, fritillaries, Paeony officianalis, and Catanache caerulea add to the period feel. As one of Major Bowen's great interests was conservation, wildflowers and food plants for endangered butterfly species have been planted in the rough grass of the orchard. This looks particularly attractive as it is bounded by a rose arch through which a path is mown, the rest of the

grass being cut only twice a year.

Beyond, at the far end of the garden is the area set out in traditional Physic or Herb beds. Between gravel paths neat beds containing over seventy varieties of plants 'for use and for delight' have been laid out by Peter Mason who was formerly curator of the Butser Iron Age Farm. Camomile (stomach-settler, v. Peter Rabbit), elecampane (bronchitis and skin trouble) and agrimony (liver) grow alongside the spicy artemisias, aromatic sages and fragrant lavenders. Herbs are also propagated for sale.

For many centuries medical knowledge was based almost entirely on plant lore and now, once again we seem to be turning to 'phytotherapy' or plant medicine. It is even coming back into the hospitals and consulting

**The Hampshire garden has been cultivated continuously for eight centuries**

A sundial has been erected in the garden as a memorial to Major J.C.E. Bowen

ferns and elms are especially detailed. He assisted Johnson, who gave him lavish credit, with the second edition of *Gerard's Herball*. One of the plants mentioned is the Jerusalem artichoke of which Goodyear says, 'I received two small roots thereof from Master Franqueuill of London, no bigger than a hen's egg... (which) brought me a peck of roots wherewith I stored Hampshire...' However, rather disconcertingly, he continues 'which way soever they be drest and eaten they stirre and cause a filthie loathsome stinking winde within the body...'! John Parkinson the King's Herbalist in his *Theatrum Botanicum* written in 1624, also pays tribute to Goodyear calling him 'A great lover and curious searcher of plants who hath found in our country many other plants not imagined to grow in our Land'. In Petersfield's new physic garden four beds are devoted to the plants associated with John Goodyear.

rooms, perhaps as a reaction from the harsh drugs of the last few decades. The Association of British Herbalists report an increase in public interest. Aromatherapy, which makes use of the healing properties of essential plant oils, is also booming. Further, modern research proves that old plants can still have modern uses. The Madagascar periwinkle which came to Chelsea in 1894, has recently been found efficacious in the treatment of leukaemia and Hodgkin's disease.

In the 17th century of course many of these plants were new for this was the great age of plant hunting and a further link is provided with this garden by the fact that John Goodyear, the famous botanist born in 1592, lived most of his life in Petersfield. He added many important plants to the British list and his descriptions of

As well as the plants used for healing and the herbs we generally associate with the kitchen, various dye plants are to be found in the physic garden. At Petersfield, Woad, traditionally associated with ancient Britons grows well. It is not such common knowledge that as late as 1939 this plant was used to dye the uniforms of the Metropolitan police.

On the far side of the garden there is a small door which leads out to a path beside a stream. This land also belonged to Major Bowen and many

years ago he planted two magnificent swamp cypresses which, although outside the garden, provide a mature element which contrasts beautifully with the texture of the Sussex knapped flint walls.

*Above:* **The bench designed by local girl, Anna Griffiths, as part of her A-level Design course**

*Below:* **To maintain the 17th-century theme, a topiary walk has been laid out**

The atmosphere within the garden is warm and welcoming, the sound of bees, the colours, flowers and butterflies and the scent of aromatic plants fills the air. The community feels involved in this garden; local W.I.s and individuals have made it gifts and there is no lack of volunteers to help. A lovely curved wooden bench designed and constructed by a 17-year old local girl, Anna Griffiths as part of her A-level Design course, stands in one corner. Paths are wide enough for wheelchairs and the sheltered garden provides a much needed amenity in which people relax, enjoying the sunshine and the plants. Major Bowen could have made a great deal of money by selling this prime site to a supermarket chain, instead it is a haven of calm. In this hurried day and age every town could do with a small garden such as this.

## Longford Mill – new developments?

LONGFORDS Mill (*Country Origins,* Spring) near Avening in Gloucestershire, has become the subject of much discussion and controversy. Hartley Property Trust, a London-based development company, have put forward a scheme for creating 73 executive homes on the site, which will incorporate some of the thirty listed buildings and involve the demolition of the more modern mill buildings. This has generated a great deal of opposition locally, including objections from Princess Anne whose estate, Gatcombe Park, is next to the Mill: Longfords Lake is sometimes called Gatcombe Water, and Gatcombe Woods are part of the setting which make it such a beautiful site. The proposal involves lowering the level of the lake, which is particularly worrying to environmental groups.

The Stroud Valleys Project and the Stroud Preservation Trust are bringing people together and trying to generate ideas for the future of the Mill – positive alternatives, which will involve public access to this much loved site. The greatest problem, perhaps, is that access to the Mill is very difficult, and if it were to be transformed into a complex of industrial museum, educational or conference centre, workshop and housing, then a new road or monorail or alternative transport would have to be built – the same, or course, would be true for an executive village.

The Stroud Valleys are a very 'Green', environmentally-conscious area, and people want the Mill to be a focus for imaginative 'Green' development, rather than just a site with more than a few problems of access, repair and maintenance. People are hopeful that Prince Charles, who lives and farms nearby at Highgrove, and who has recently taken up the cause of disused industrial buildings, will also become involved. –
*Jacqueline Sarsby*

# Questions and Answers

*Do you need help, advice, others to work with? Then this section is for you. So what do you do to get help? Firstly decide if it is a question you would like answered in the magazine on this page, and if so send your question to Questions and Answers, Country Origins, PO Box 4, Nairn IV12 4HU, or if you have a computer and a modem you can leave it on the Bulletin Board on 01443–475900.*

When I was a child visiting my grandmother in mid Wales during the holidays, I would play with my dolls and teddy bears and use the item in the above picture as a seat and sometimes a bed. I am sure it must have had a more practical purpose, but I never really found out, do you have any idea?

From our sources the only item I have been able to find that is similar to this was amongst some bakery items in a local museum. It is what the Welsh would call an Oakdale Rack. It is made of wood and was used during the 19th century to dry out the oatcakes that had been baked that day.

**I have been trying to track down the birth certificate of my great grandfather Edward Smith who I believe was born in 1877 in Northampton, but a look on the index at my local Mormon Centre proves a nightmare as there are a number of entries for this name in this year. Unfortunately, as far as I know, he was not given another name. What can I do, as I am reluctant to go to the expense of getting a number of certificates in order to track down the right one.**

It is difficult when there are multiple entries of the same name in the index. First of all of course you can rule out those that have a second name, assuming he did only have one Christian name. Now from those that are left you will probably find that Northampton, being a large area, was split into a number of sub-districts. Using old maps and maps of the registration districts see if you can identify which sub-district he was likely to be in. Alternatively if he had any brothers or sisters see if you can track down their details and check if anything is common. Finally you could visit the local registry office and look at their indexes or ask to see the original books for the period in which you are interested. They will charge you a fee but at least you are able to see the parents' names and other details before purchasing the certificate.

**Recently I was helping a friend, whose grandfather had just passed away, to clear out an old shed. We came across an item in an old box which was a bit rusted up, but looked as though it could have once been a type of bell. It is made of a metal and has a long handle with a hoop on it, presumably for hanging it up. The largest part is cylindrical which has a little peep hole on one side and inside it appears to be empty. The top end of the cylinder is flat and sealed off with another hook at the other end. Was it a bell?**

From the description you have given us and the diagram included in your letter we have been able to locate a photograph which I think is the item you are describing. It is in fact a cooking item, made of brass, called a Spinning Jack. You can see from the photograph that it is hooked on to a serrated lever. This hangs on the wall above the fireplace where the cooking would have been done, the different positions allowing it to be placed either closer to or further away from the fire. Inside the cylindrical piece is a clockwork mechanism and the little peep hole was where you would set the clock going. The hook on the bottom would have held the piece of meat and the clockwork mechanism inside would spin the meat while it was cooking over the fire.

**My ancestors were Congregationalists; how can I find out more about this religious group and possibly details on my family's involvement?**

The Congregationalists derived from the Brownists who were followers of Robert Browne back in the late 1500s. They were also known as independents and believed that the state should not interfere in religious matters. They expanded substantially during the 19th century and in 1831 the Congregationalists Union of England and Wales was formed. The first known date of a register of their members dates from 1644 and in 1840 all known surviving registers were deposited at the Public Record Office in London. There is a Congregational Library in Farringdon Street, London EC4 and they hold such things as church rolls,

various books and manuscripts, minutes books of congregations, committees and associations and various collections. The Congregational Federation at 4 Castle Gate, Nottingham NG1 7AS may also be able to help you.

**While looking through the 1861 census for one of my ancestors I came across the term Coastermonger in the occupation column, can you identify what this may have been?**

A coastermonger was a term first used to describe someone who sold apples. However it later became a term to describe someone who sold fruit and vegetables from a barrow.

**I recently purchased a country farm and had to sort through a number of old barns and sheds ready for my own use when I came across the item in the photograph. I assume it's an agricultural tool, but do you know what it is?**

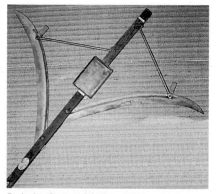

It is in fact a thistle cutter which was towed by a horse. The box type container in the middle would have had

weights put in it to give it an even balance. As the horse pulled it through the thistles the blades on either side would cut them down to an even depth.

**I'm doing a project looking at the animals on the farm around the time of World War 2. Is there any information which might help me with my project?**

Although *Black's Veterinary Dictionary* is in its 18th edition, it has been published since 1928. You may be able to get hold of a copy in a good second hand book shop. You should certainly find it very helpful with your project.

**Why were ladies' undergarments known as bloomers?**

The name is derived from an American feminist whose name was Amelia Jenks Bloomer (1818–1894). The original bloomer outfit was a lot different from what we think of as bloomers today. It was controversial in its day because at that time it was only considered that men should wear trousers. But Amelia introduced an all-in-one garment based on a design created by a lady called Elizabeth Smith Miller.

It was a full costume consisting of a loose fitting tunic, a short knee length skirt and billowing trousers gathered at the ankle, whereas later the undergarment only had the billowing trousers and was elasticated at the knee. During the 19th century the word became associated with a knee-length garment worn by cyclists and then later referred to ladies' undergarments.

# Then and Now

MANY times when we look at changes that have taken place we compare photographs taken at the beginning of the century with recent ones, and see not only a change of buildings but a total change of life. In this issue we have instead chosen three views taken within a single country village in the 1960s, and looked at the same views today.

The village we have chosen for this exercise is Purton, in the north of Wiltshire. It is a village around six miles north west of Swindon, and has a history going back to well before the Domesday book. Many notable people in history have come from this village, and historically it shows signs going back to the New Stone Age having a hill fort (earthworks) to the west and a lot of Roman coins and other items having been found in the area. It has never had any great industries being mainly a farming area, and more recently, a dormitory for Swindon which, although now one of the fastest growing towns in Europe, was a very small village before the railway came.

In the 60s, it was a striving and popular village, with solid countryside and had a number of villages between it and Swindon. It had a brickworks and a few small businesses. There had been the addition recently of a new arcade of around six shops, which was built where previously there had been a farm and a riding school. A secondary modern school had recently been built for the children of the village and for pupils from villages and towns to the north, who would travel daily by bus. The village had a church and two Methodist chapels, and several hundred active organisations, a mental hospital, and an old people's home.

So what has happened since? Swindon has grown and although there are still a few fields between Purton and Swindon, the encroaching developments are now visible. The villages in between have just about all been swallowed up, although some of their names remain, amongst the many new named places to appear. The brickyard has closed, one of the chapels has been converted to a house, a lot more houses have been built, both in the form of estates and infill in all the gaps, and some behind in what were formerly long gardens. The mental hospital has been demolished and the sight redeveloped to contain a health centre and some other facilities as well. The old people's home was also demolished and a smaller one built on part of the site, and the remainder sold for housing. A sheltered housing complex and pensioner's bungalows have been built. The school has grown very much larger and of course become comprehensive. The station closed many years ago, and the vicarage is now a hotel.

The many old houses of the area appear the same, although some have had their outbuildings converted to homes, the tithe barn the unusual church with both a tower and spire and the toll house appear largely

unchanged.

Throughout history the village has changed, originally starting as a cluster of manors, with most of the early development around the church. As communications and roads became more important the majority of the development moved a little to the north and became a long thin ribbon development along the main road, that joined Wootton Bassett one way and Cricklade the other. Further developments occurred in spurts until the 50s but since then development has been more intense.

The first photograph shows a view in the 60s down the main road, the wall on the right is the wall around

the mental hospital. The same view today shows a similar situation. On the right, the wall has gone, the scout hall, an old chapel before, has been replaced, the copse of beech trees cut down. Just the other side of the phone box, although now not as prominent as when they were built, is a line of old people's bungalows. On the left you can see one infill house, but there are others set further back, next to it, while when the 60s photograph was taken this area was used for chickens.

The second 60s photograph, shows the workmen's institute built in 1878 and the view down station road. Now we see that the building is

a library and museum. In the older photograph you can see a large garden behind, while now in the grounds behind it and adjoining, is a large village hall. Station road is now more developed with fields or gaps now filled in with additional housing.

The final pair is of Restrop House on the edge of the village, and although the house has changed hands several times, it remains hardly changed. However notice that two trees have gone, and new bushes or trees have been grown in the front. Legend has it that there is a secret tunnel from the cellars of this house to the church around a mile and a half away, and one previous owner said that there were signs of a tunnel although much of it has caved in.

# YOUR TOWN OR VILLAGE HAS A HISTORY

There is an enormous interest in past events from locals, nationals and even visitors from abroad. People are intrigued with the beginnings of a community, how it evolved, who lived there and how it got its name. Why not enshrine that history in print and at the same time make a profit from your enterprise?

Manuscript ReSearch (Printing Division) can not only put you on the path to success but guide your steps along the way. Send a 9" × 6" s.a.e. for our free booklet:

## *"Profit from Self-Publishing"*

This will demonstrate how you need to sell comparatively few books to make a profit, and, of course, the more you sell the greater the reward. We also provide free-of-charge continuous customer support Service to help you publish and market your book.

If the idea appeals to you and you would like to see how others have successfully undertaken this exciting venture we will send you, for £5.50 post free, an example of our work in a book portraying the Oxfordshire Village of Kirtlington, entitled:

## *"KIRTLINGTON – An Historical Miscellany"*
Edited by Henry Shellard.

---

# ORDER FORM
To: **Manuscript ReSearch Printing,**
**P.O. Box 33, Bicester, Oxon, OX6 7PP**

Please send me:
*"Profit from Self-Publishing"* .................................................. FREE
*"Kirtlington – An Historical Miscellany"*
@ £5.50 each, post free (Qty:    ) ........................................ _____
TOTAL  £ _____

(*Make cheques/postal orders payable to:* J. C. Thompson)

Name ...................................................................................................

Address ...............................................................................................

.................................................... Postcode ........................................

# Where is this?

From a collection of glass slides acquired by Andrew Gill comes this delightful scene of a horse drinking at a mill pond. The first reader to identify the location will receive a superb sepia copy 16 x 12in. Send your reply to Where is this? Autumn Country Origins, PO Box 4, Nairn IV12 4HU and enclose a sae if you want any photograph you send to be returned.

## Reader offer

Sepia copies of this photograph are available as an exclusive offer to *Country Origins* readers. Each photograph is individually hand-printed, using the finest materials and is ready for framing. Choose from two sizes: 10 x 8in for £7.95 or 16 x 12in for £12.50 per print. You can order as many as you like and the postage and packing is just £2, regardless of the quantity and size ordered.

Cheques should be made payable to 'Magic Lantern Images' and orders sent to Magic Lantern Images Offer, Country Origins (Autumn 96), PO Box 4, Nairn IV12 4HU. Please note that sizes are approximate and you should allow 28 days for delivery.